Portraits

by

A.I.

NONSUCH MEDIA PTE. LTD.

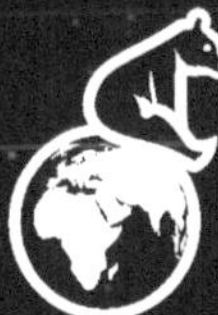

H. Matsumoto

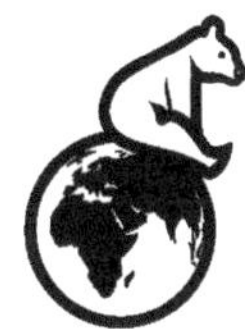

ISBN: 978-1-954145-87-0

First edition published in 2022.

Title: Portraits by A.I.
Author: H. Matsumoto
Editor: A. Lee
Images: Ji-Hoon Chow

Introduction

The first question is, are these images considered art? The pictures presented here are indeed art, even good art at that. If you are still skeptical, have a look at the following pages.

Second, the vital question is, how will this affect today's working artists? Here, the answer is more optimistic if you use it as inspiration for your own work and as an opportunity for experimentation. However, if you are only a simple executioner without much talent, your days are numbered.

The future of creativity is Artificial Intelligence (A.I.), and it is changing the way we think about art forever. Artists can now create pieces that were once only achievable through extensive hours spent mastering traditional techniques. Sometimes all you need is one good idea, and there's no telling what will come next. The use of A.I. has pushed the boundaries of artistic expression, encouraging people to experiment and collaborate in ways they may never have before.

By harnessing the machine-learning tools of recent years and combining them with our existing capabilities, we explore what a human-machine symbiosis could look like in art. This playful investigation into the possibilities excites us to consider how Artificial Intelligence may soon be an active collaborator rather than simply computing instructions. We hope these artistic creations will serve as conduits for promoting thoughtful consideration of this emerging relationship between humans and intelligent machines, making way for more creative futures.

With technology constantly evolving, we are now witnessing an unparalleled shift in the art world. With generative A.I. tools now at everyone's fingertips, imaginative artwork that would not have been possible before is being created. However, it still relies heavily on a human curator to judge what constitutes "good" or "bad." With this creative movement continuing to grow and gain momentum, we may soon see even more sophisticated fine artworks. So be prepared; there will come a time when museums celebrate remarkable achievements by Artificial Intelligence!

Through the images in this book, we hope to bring light and inspire you on how Artificial Intelligence can be used as a tool that can assist and enhance creativity.

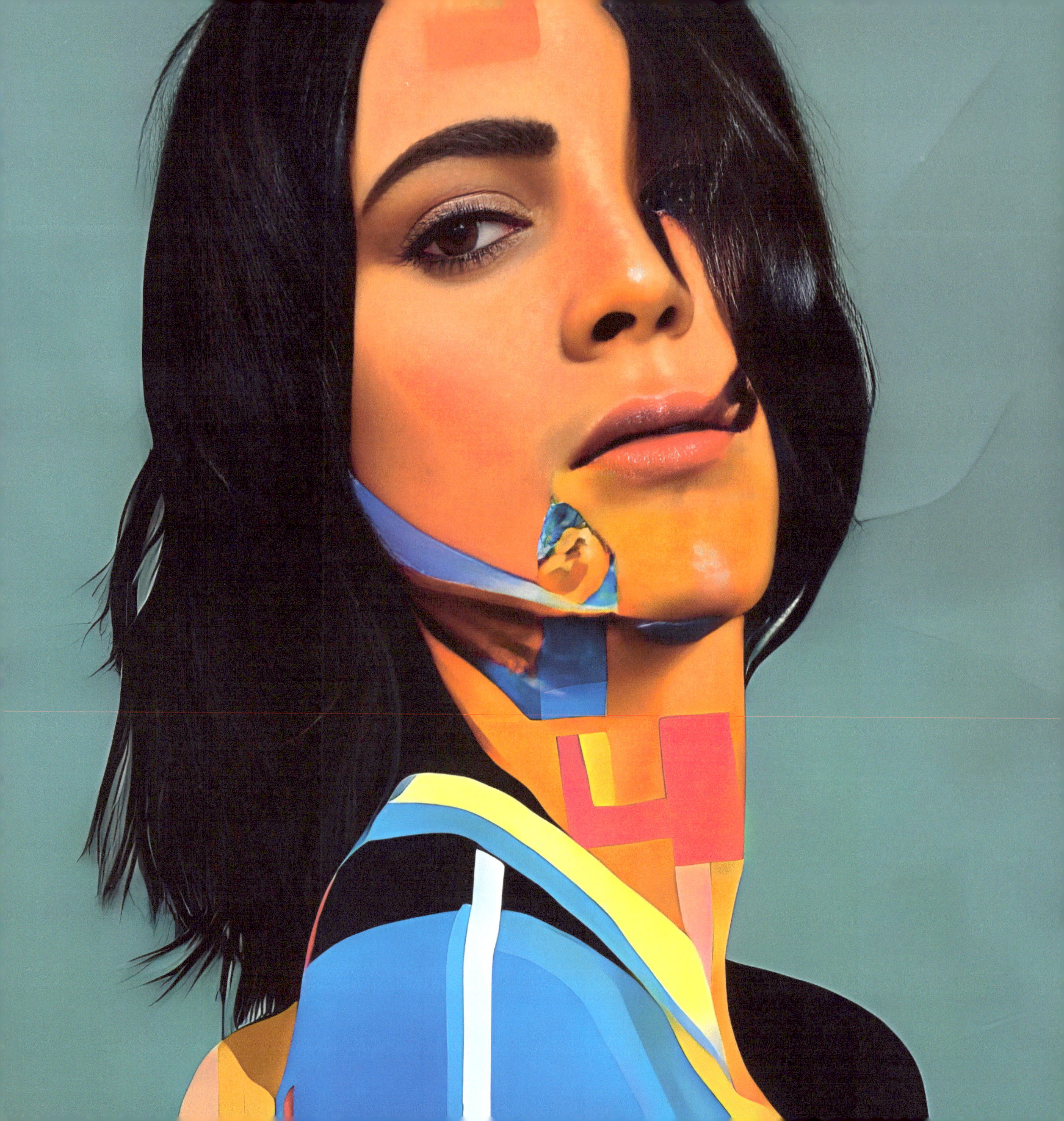

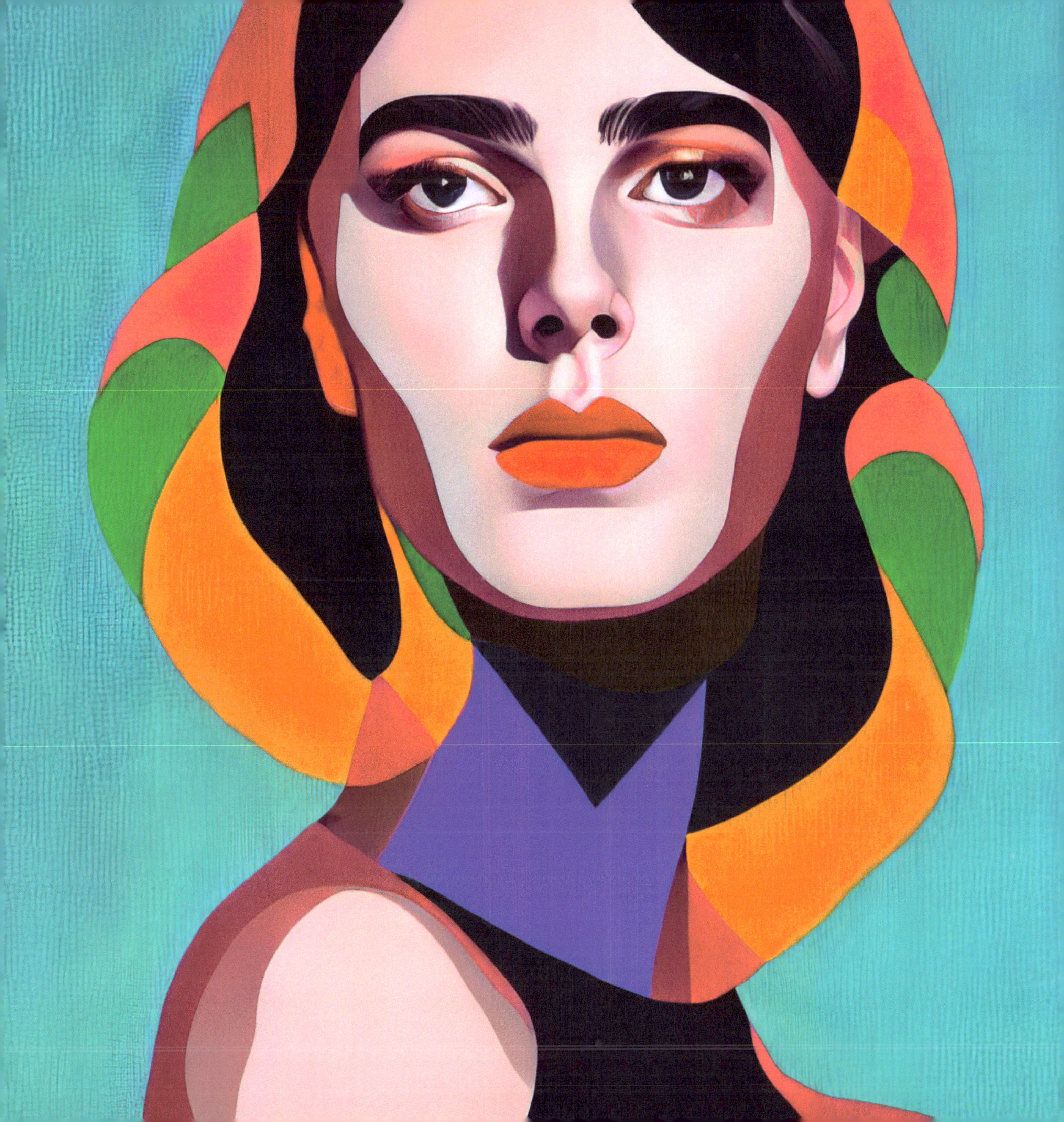

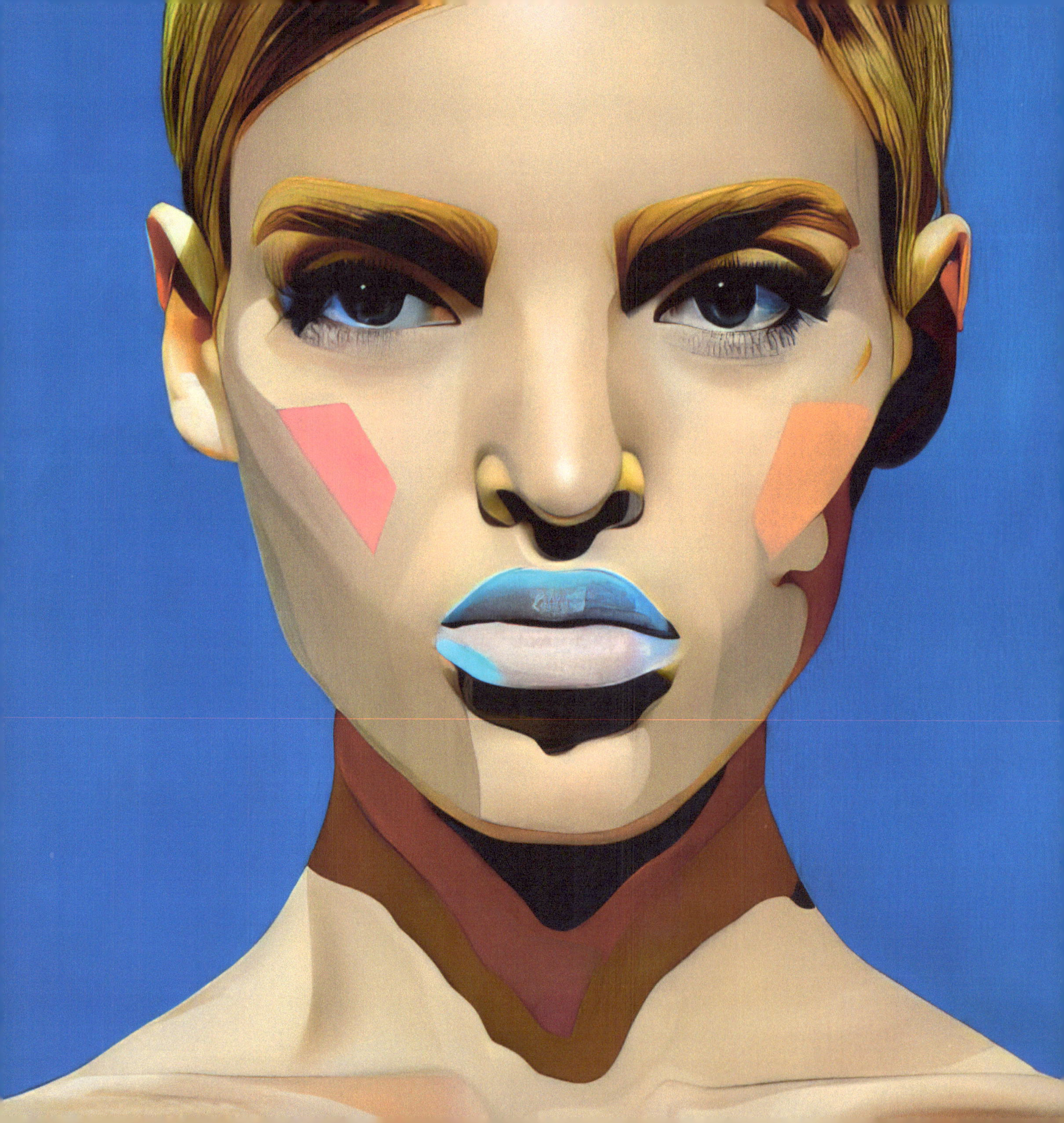

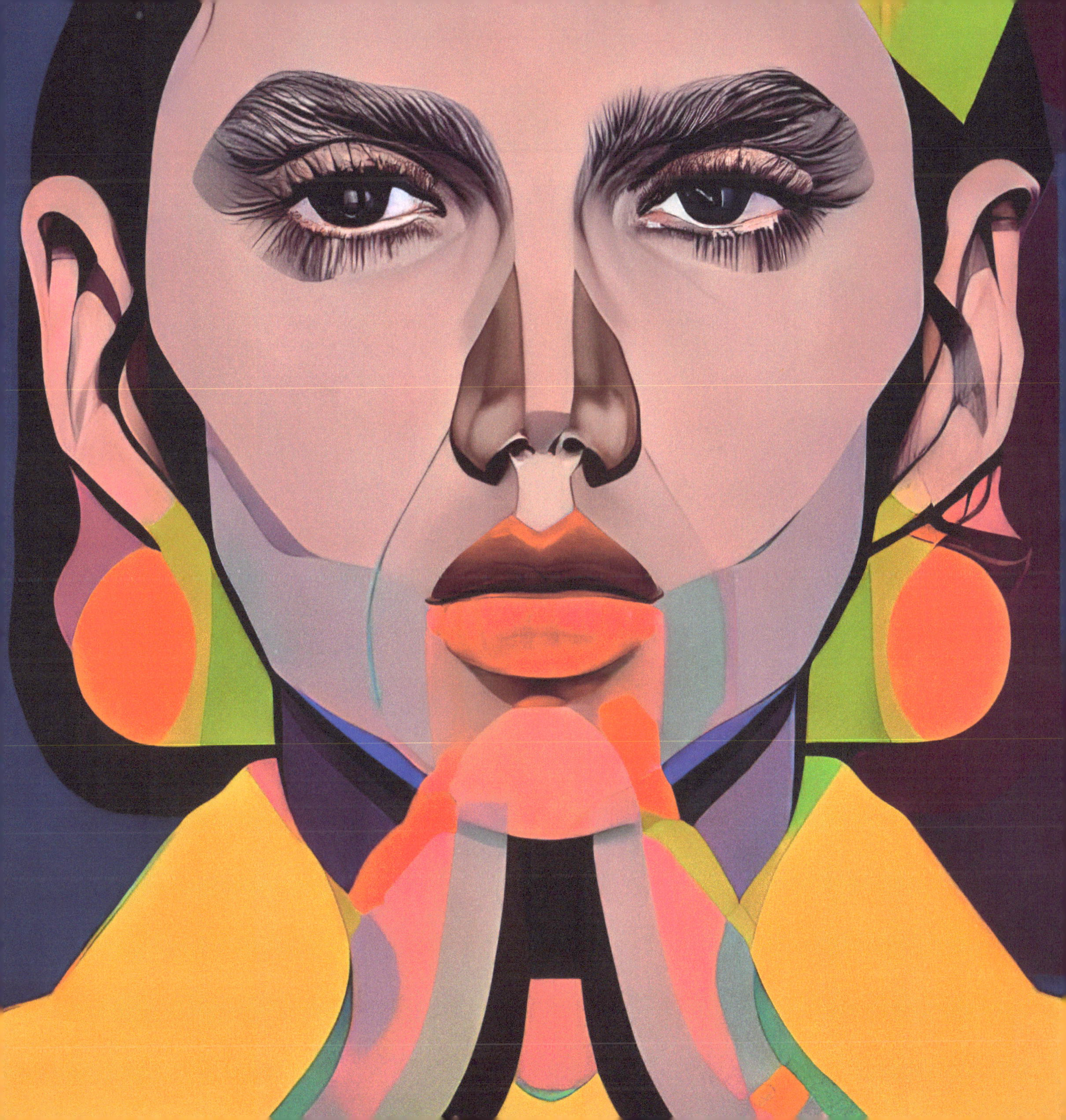

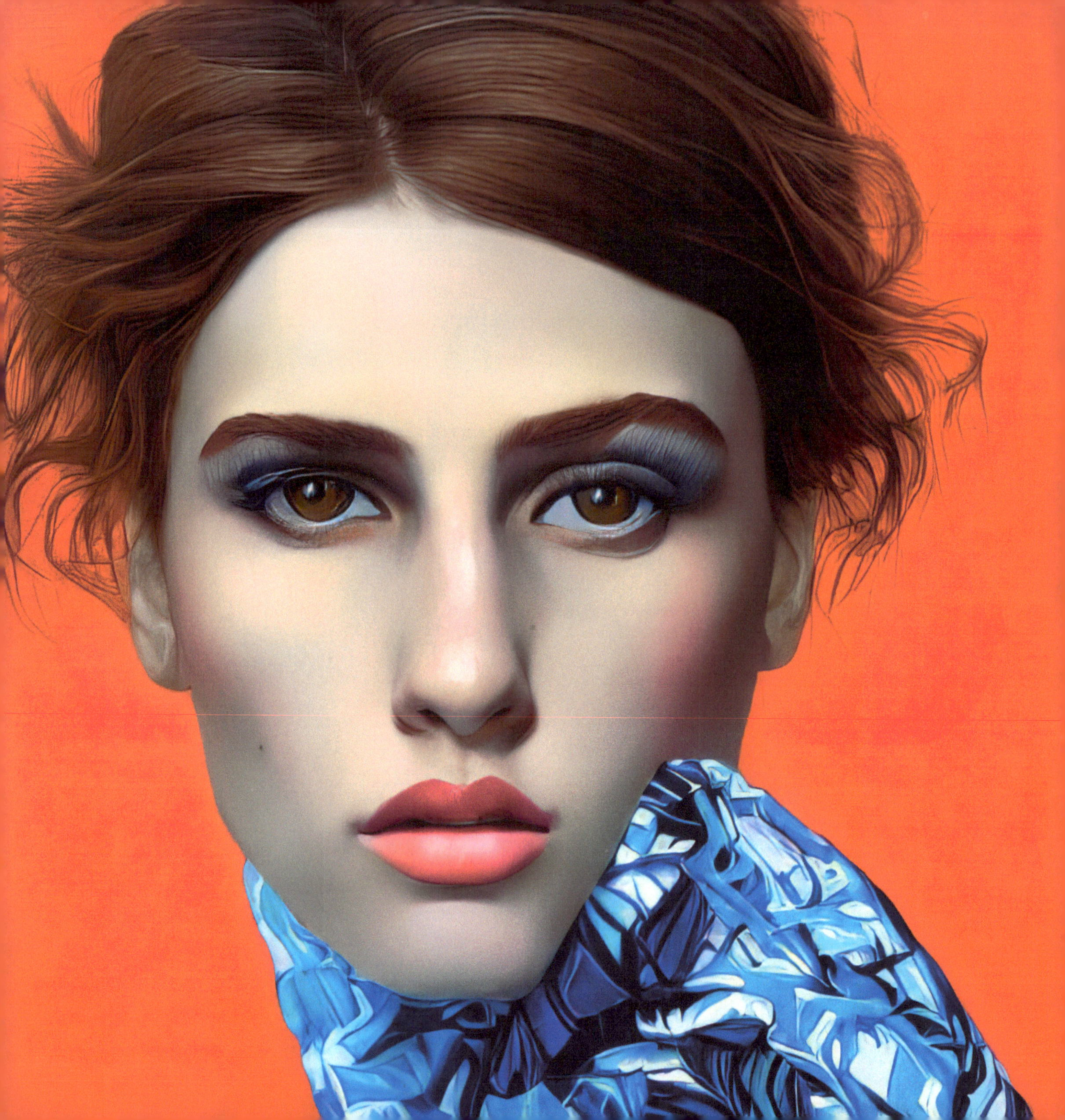

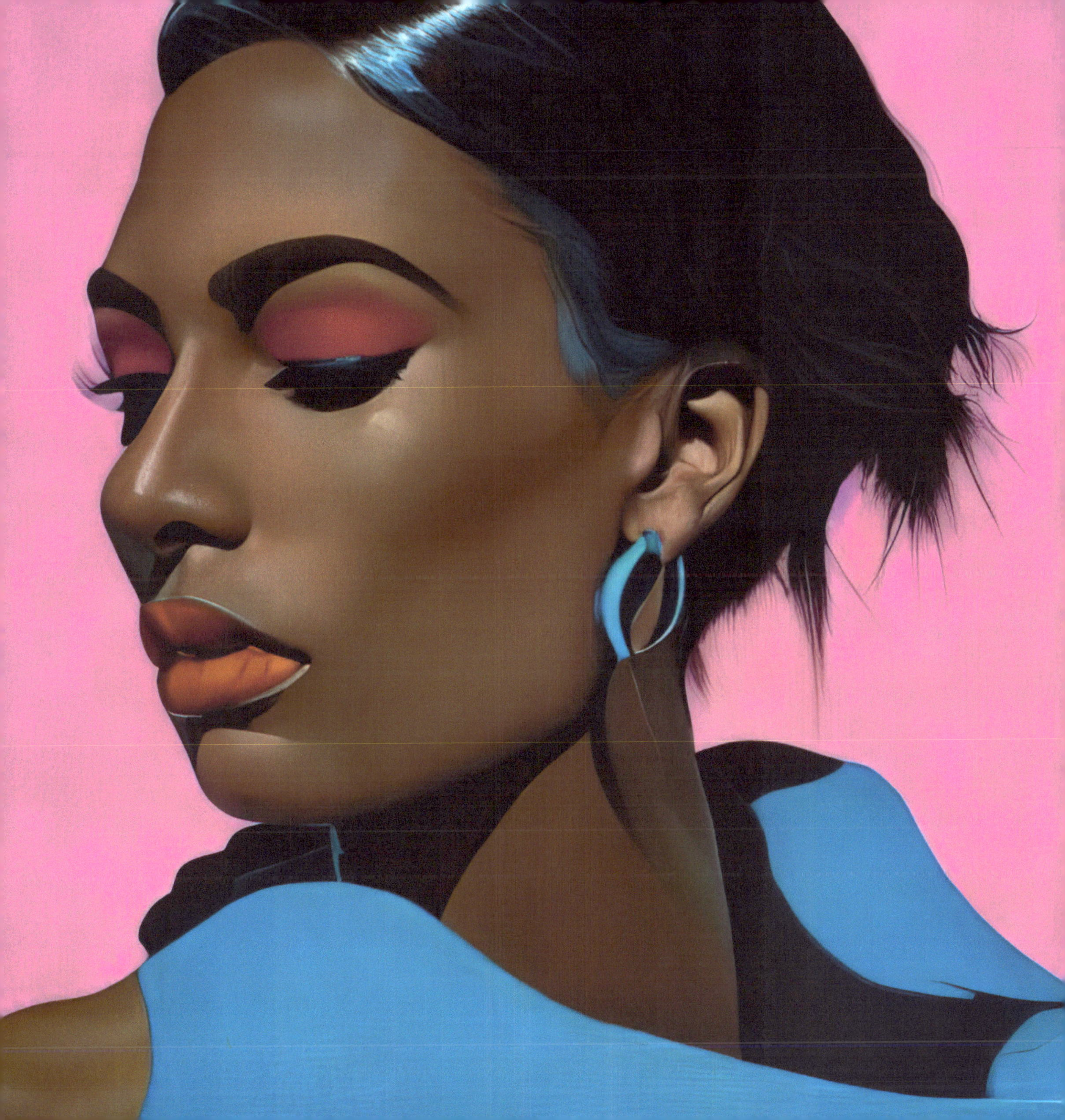

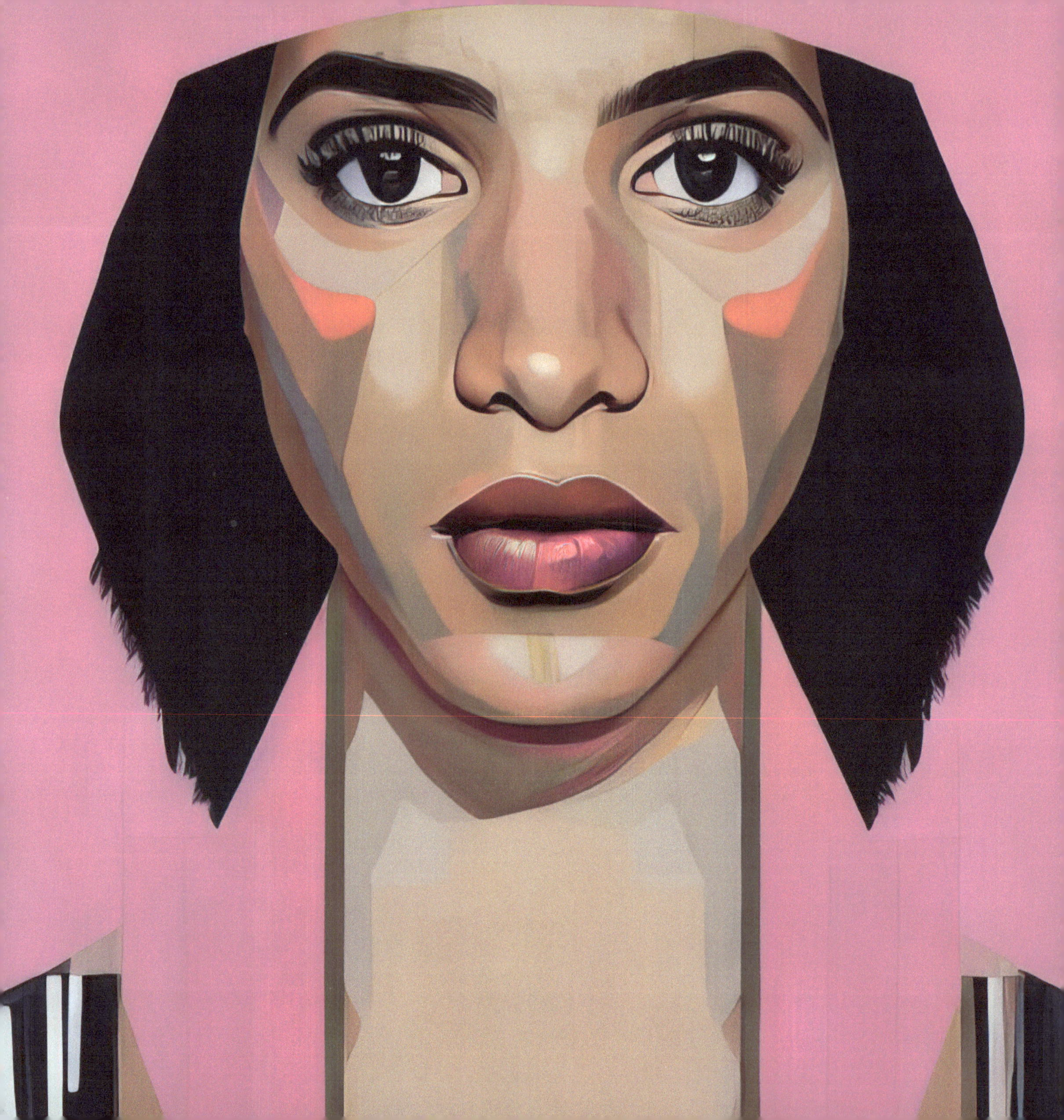

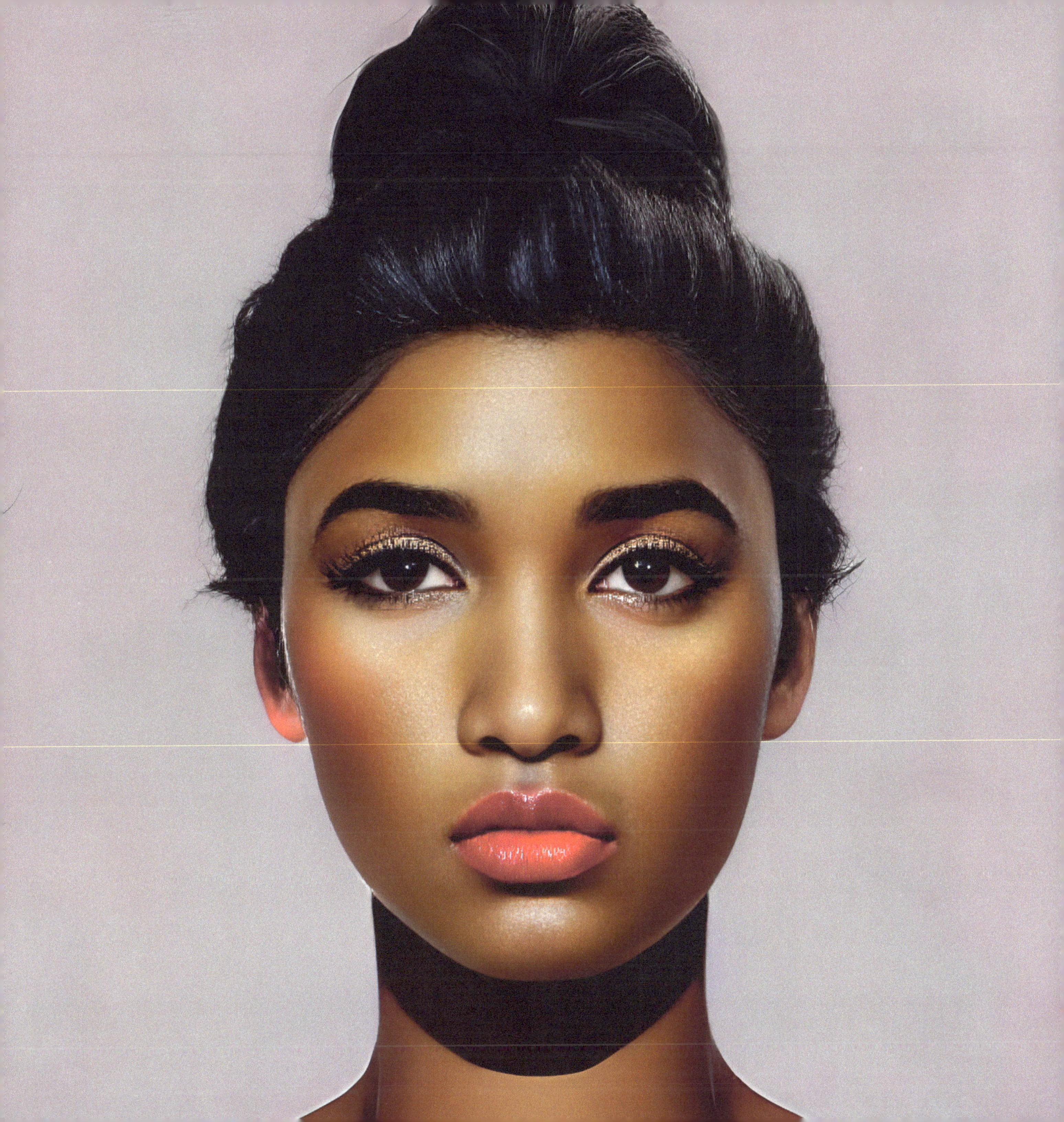

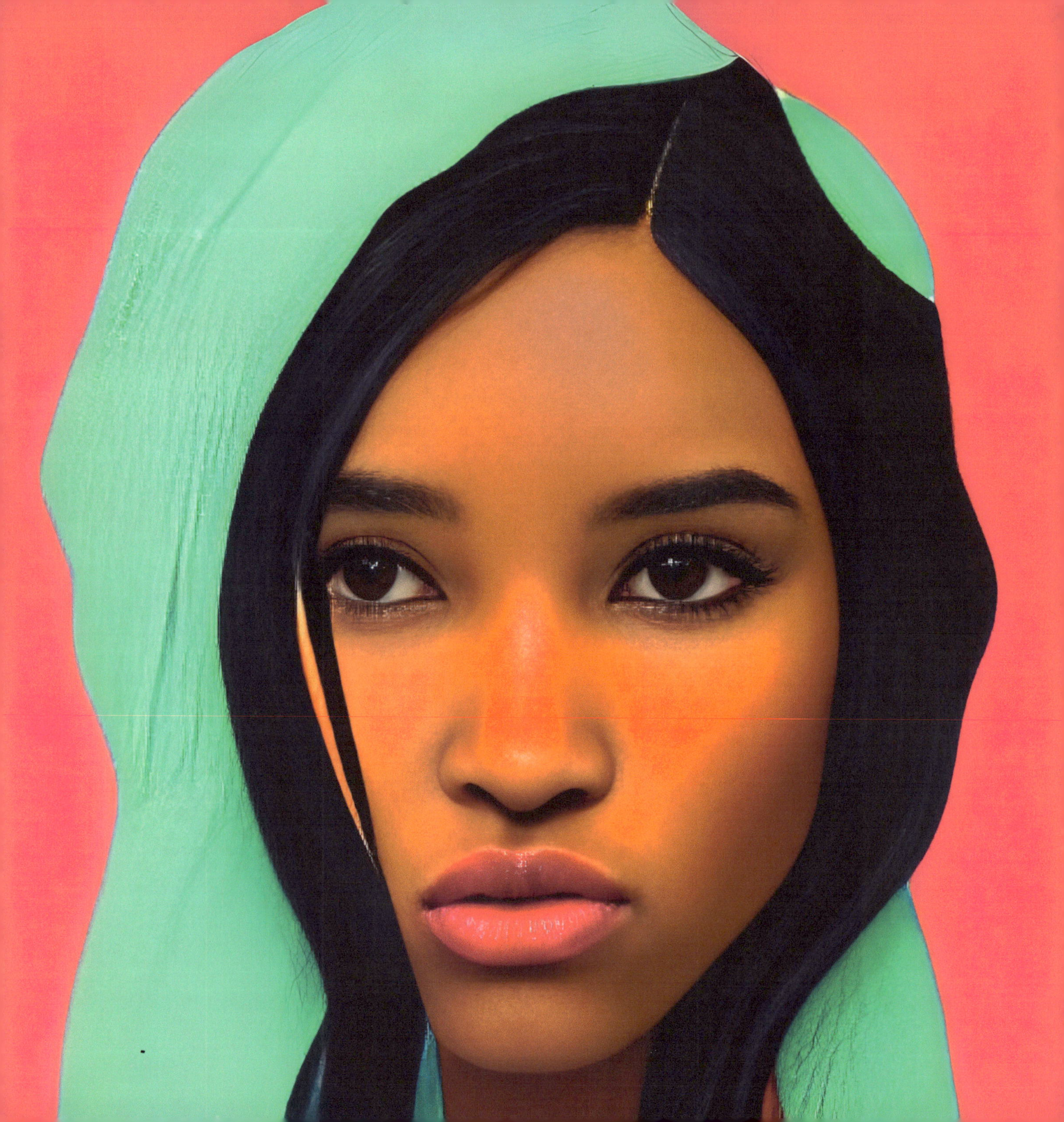

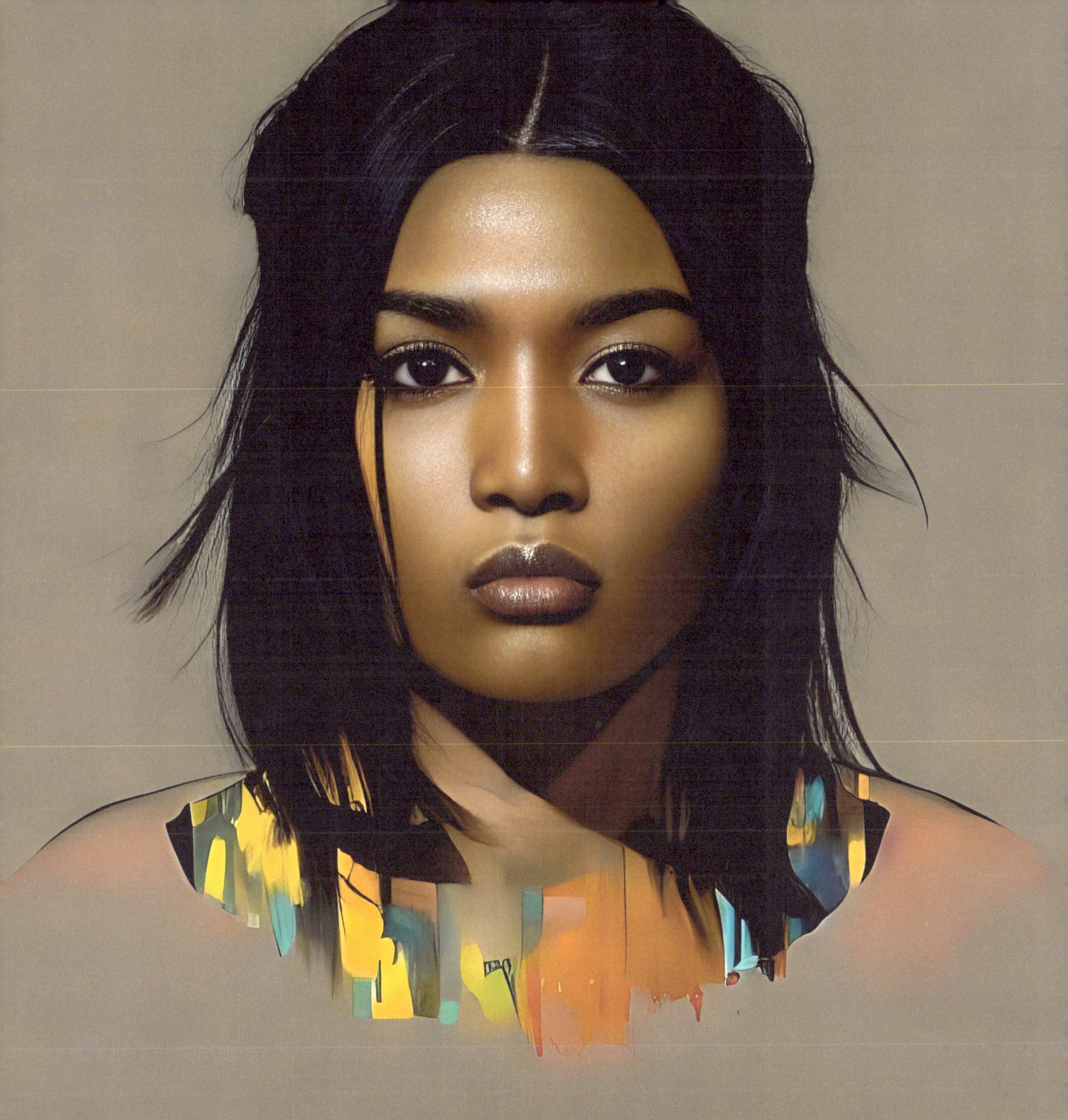

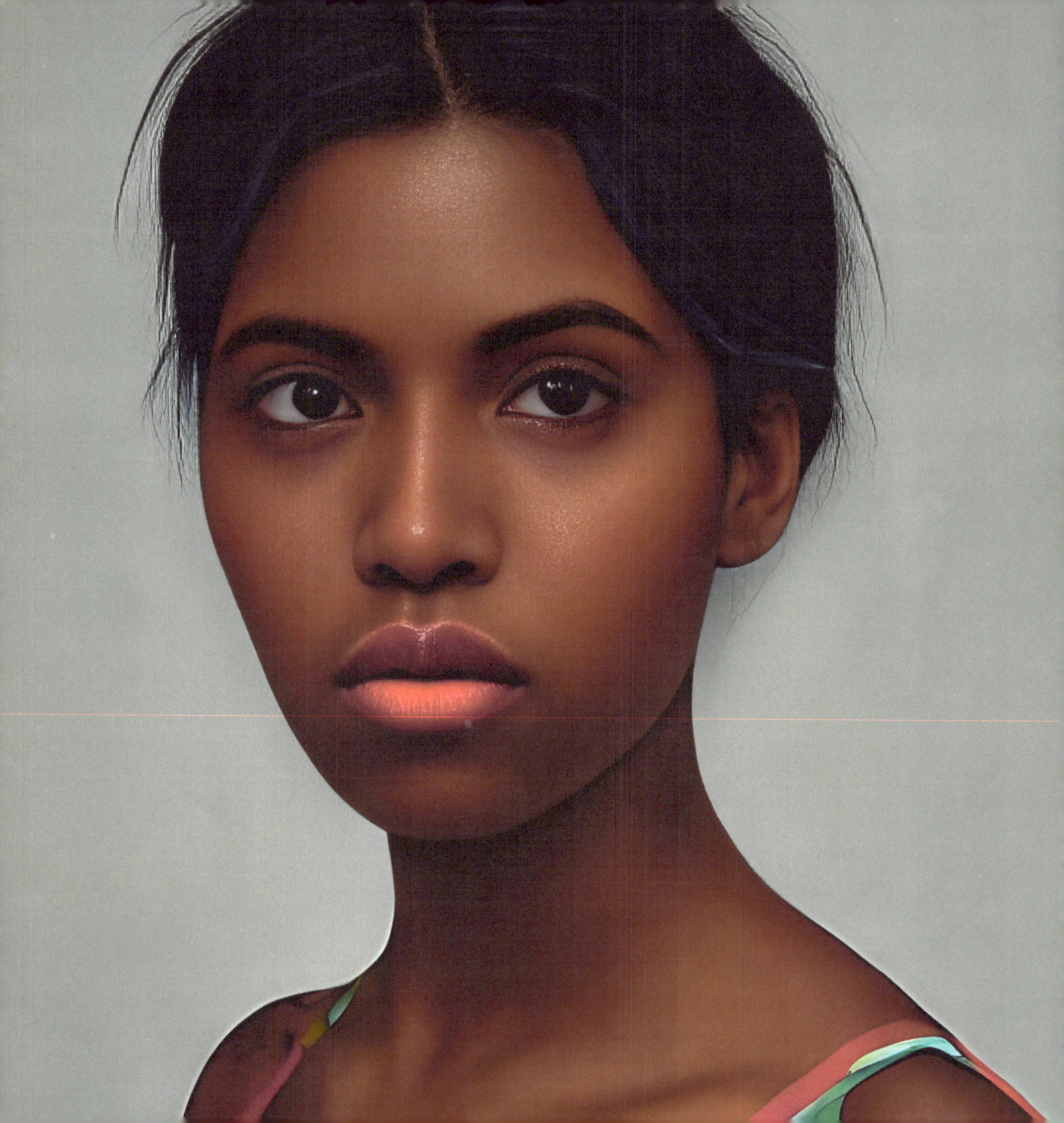

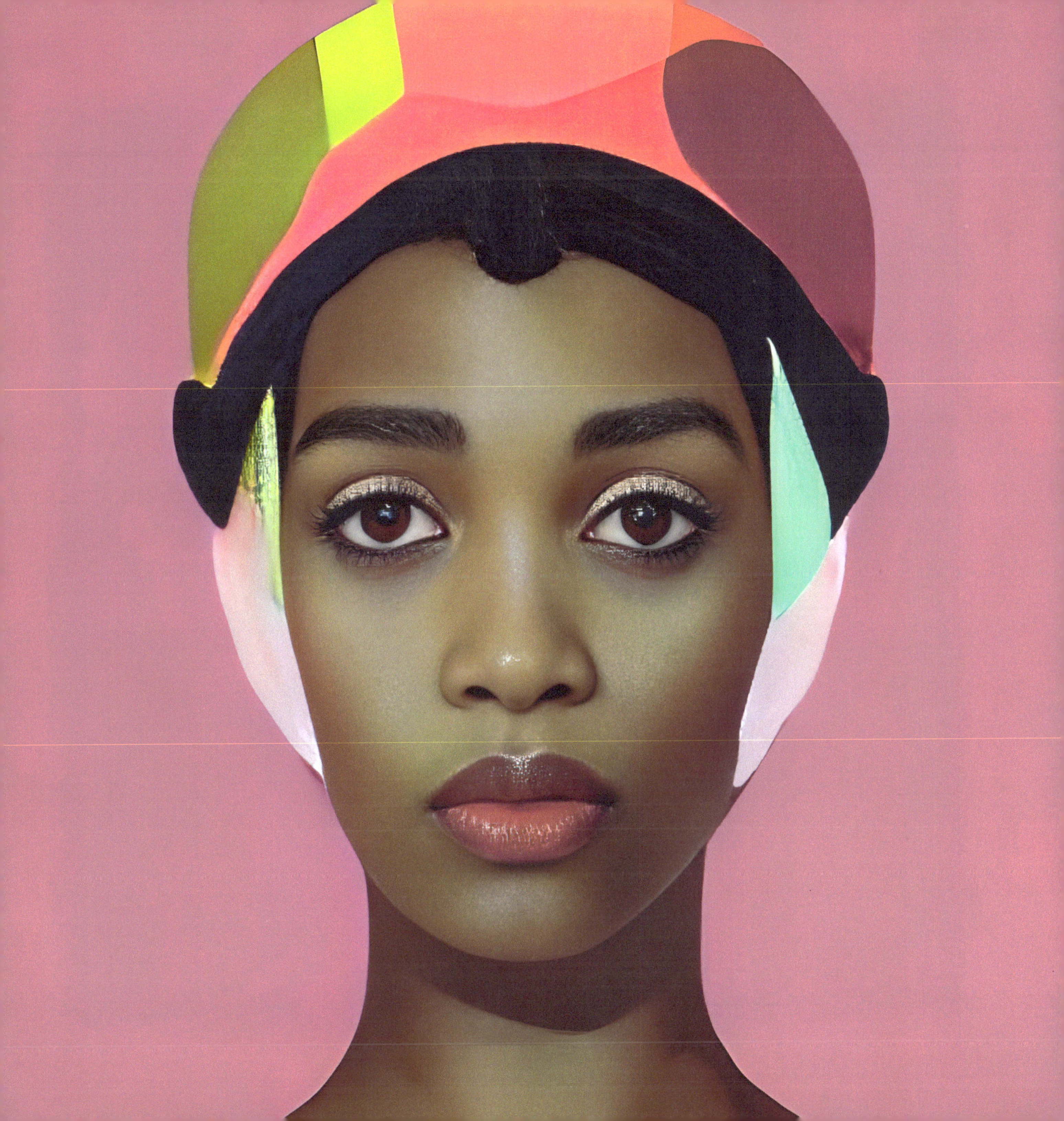

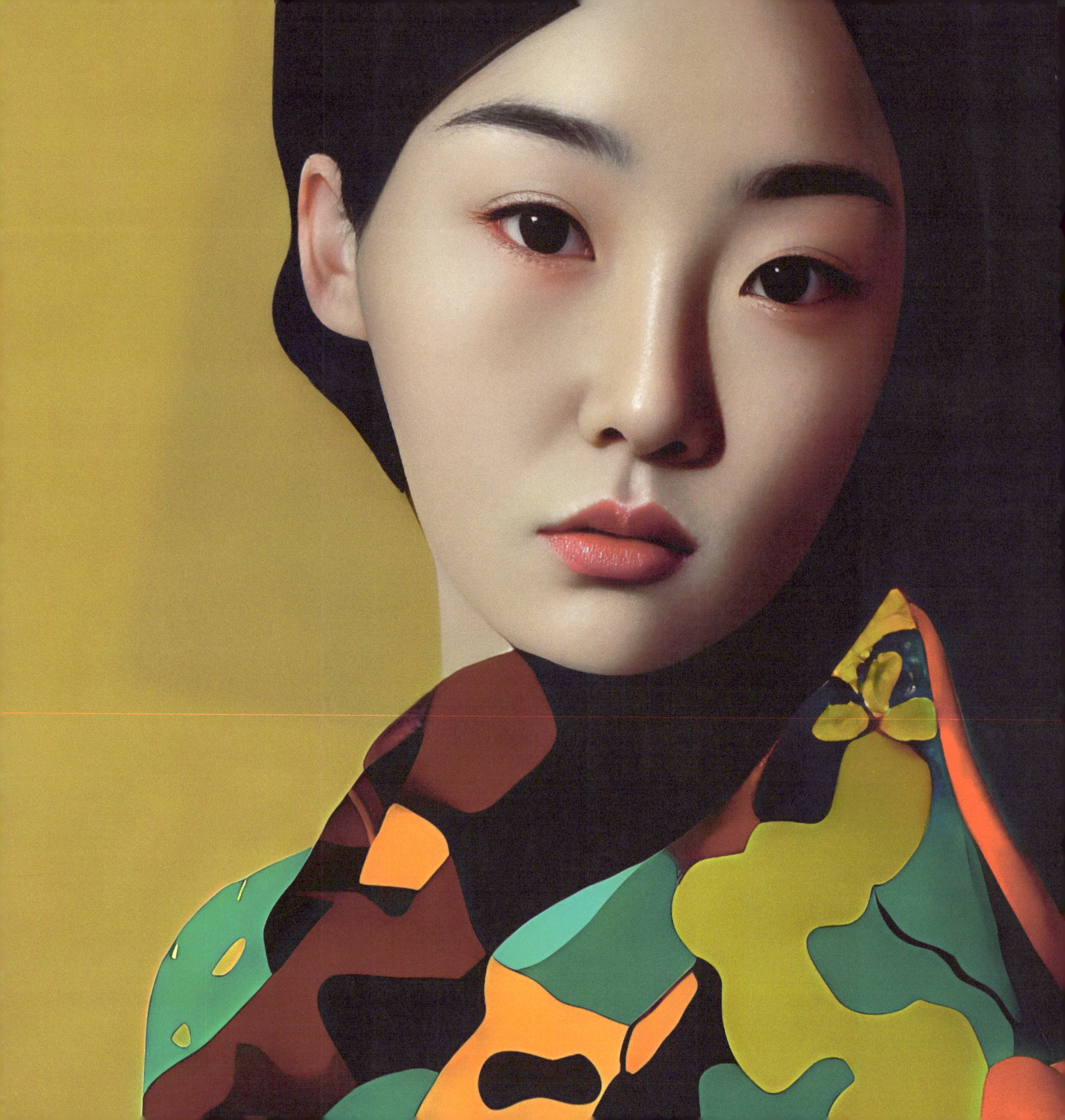

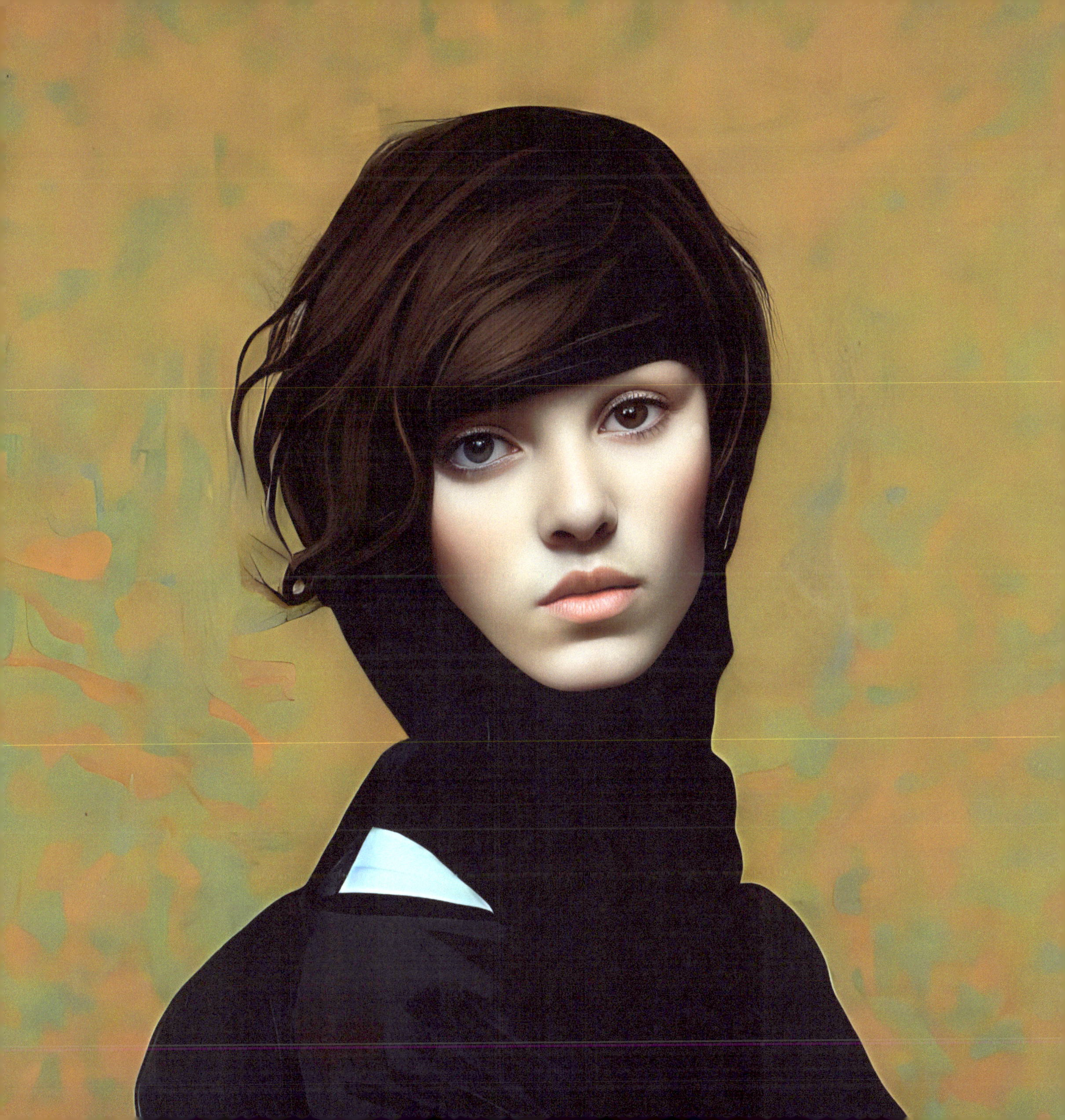

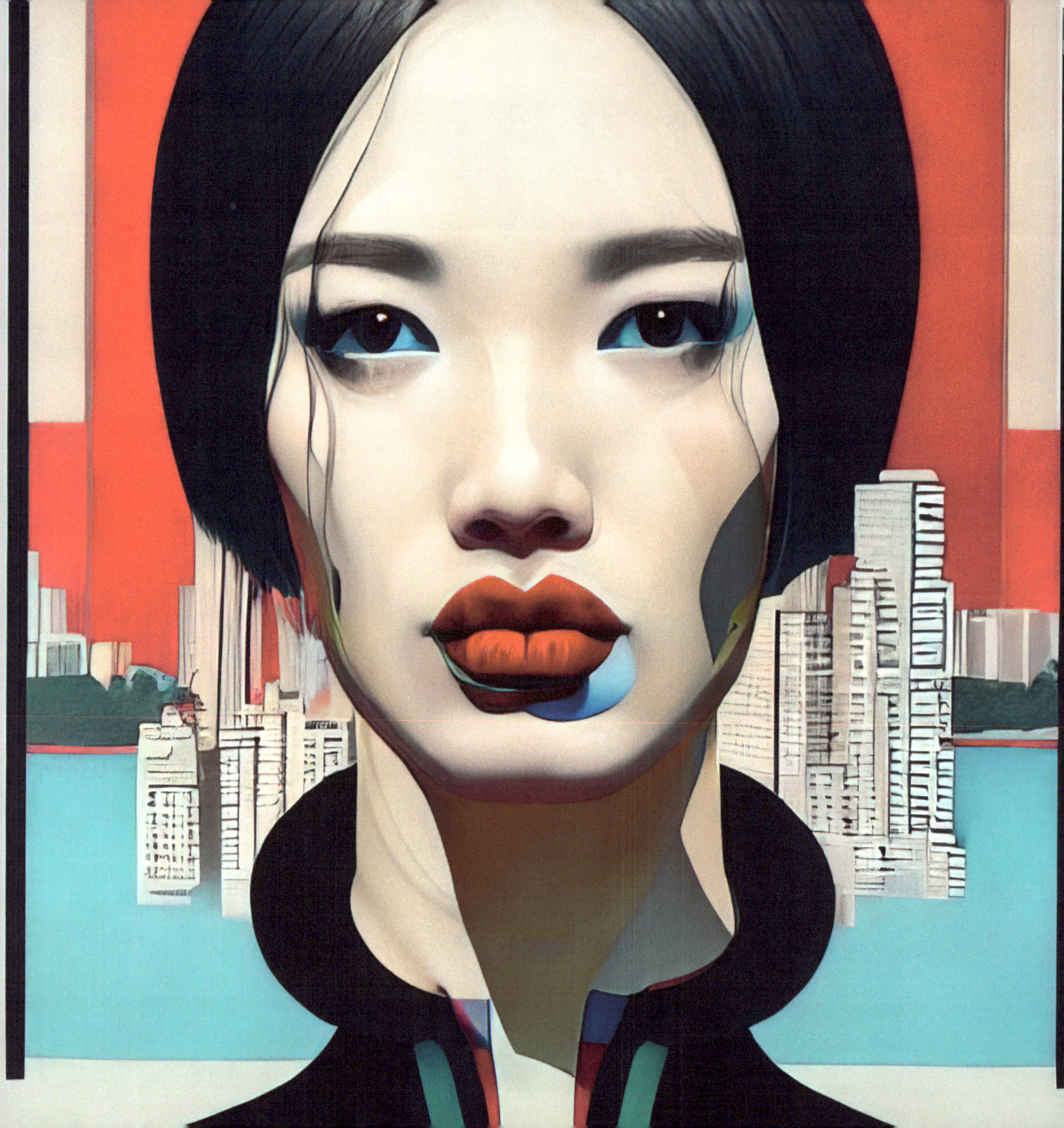

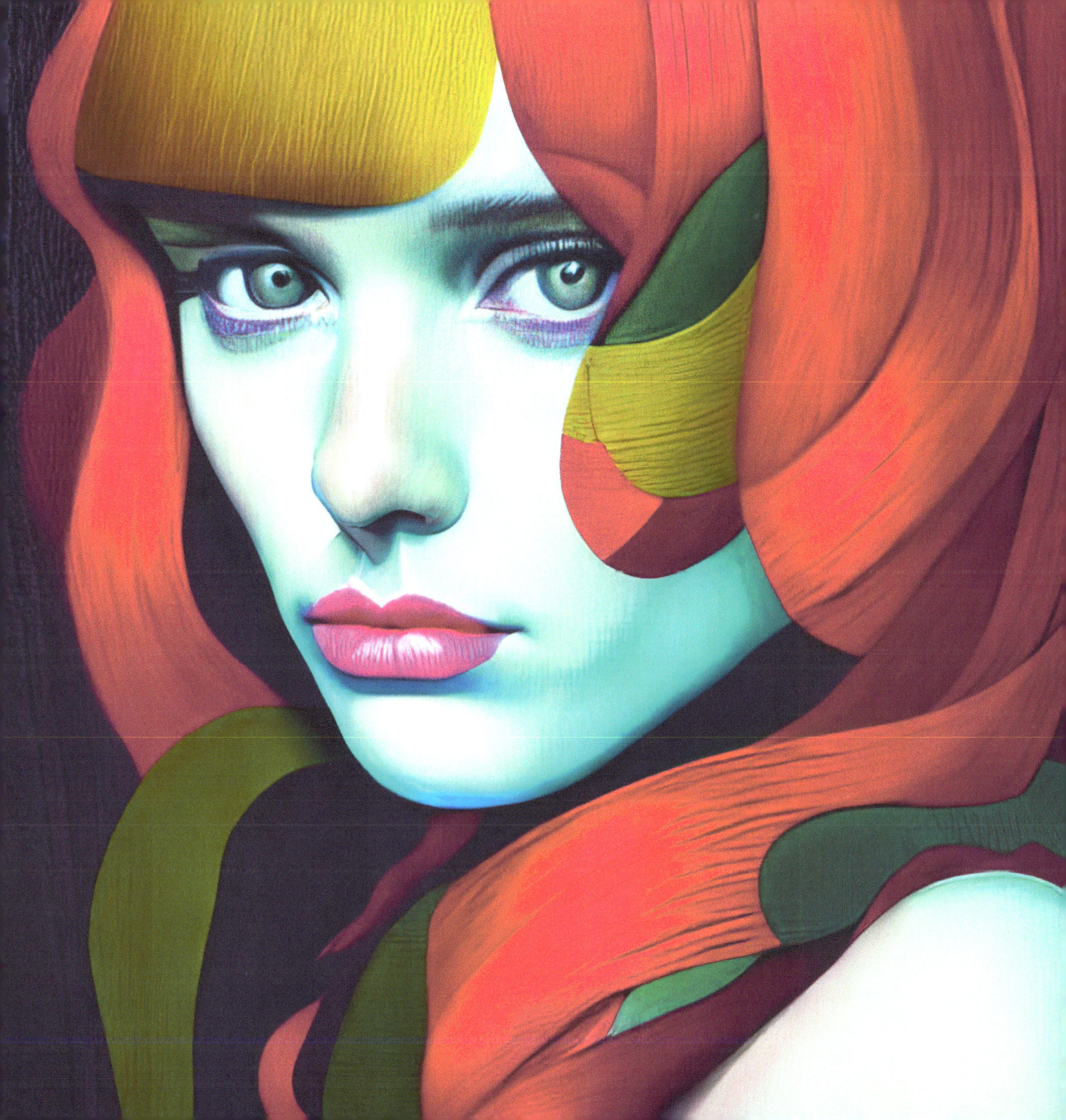

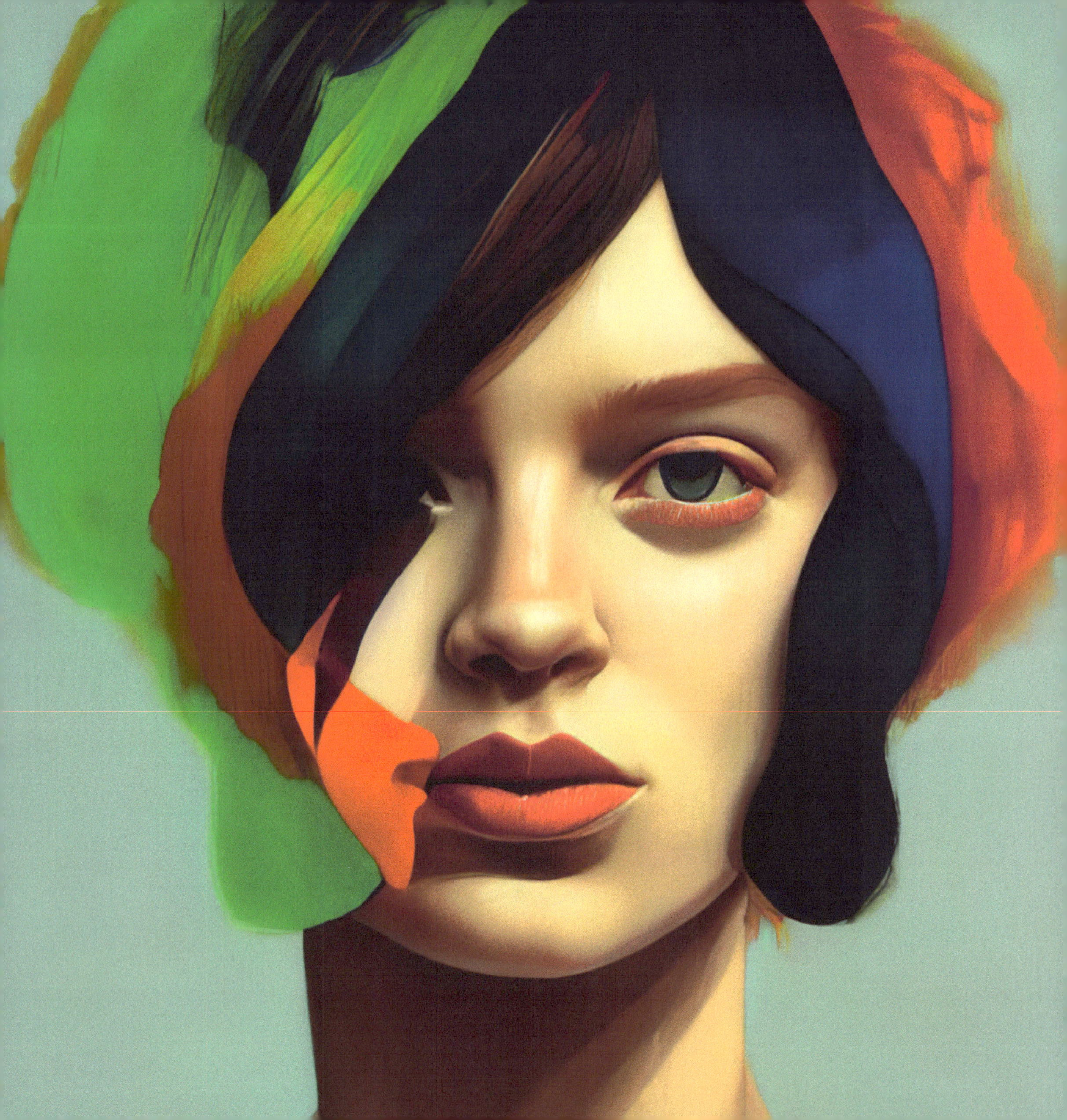

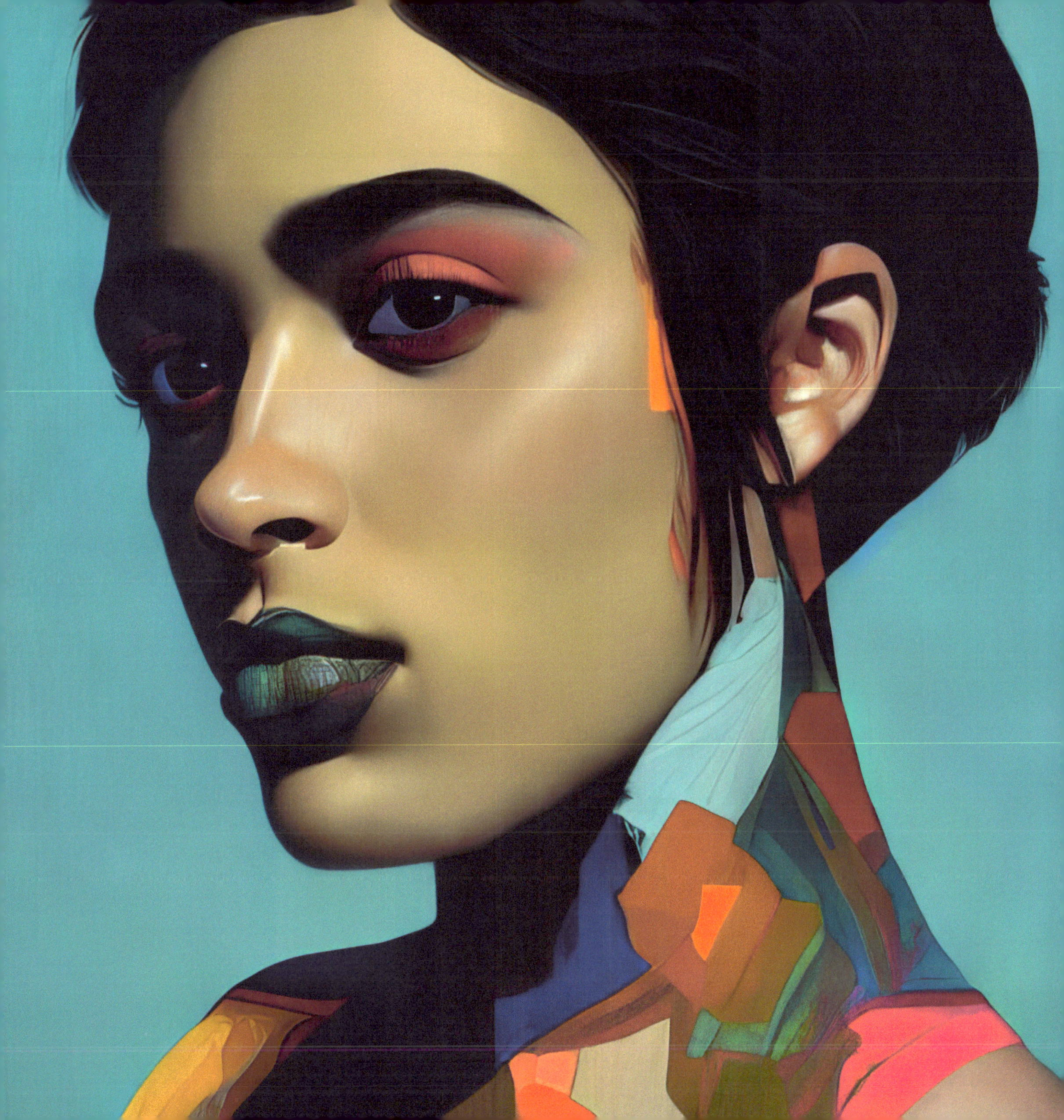

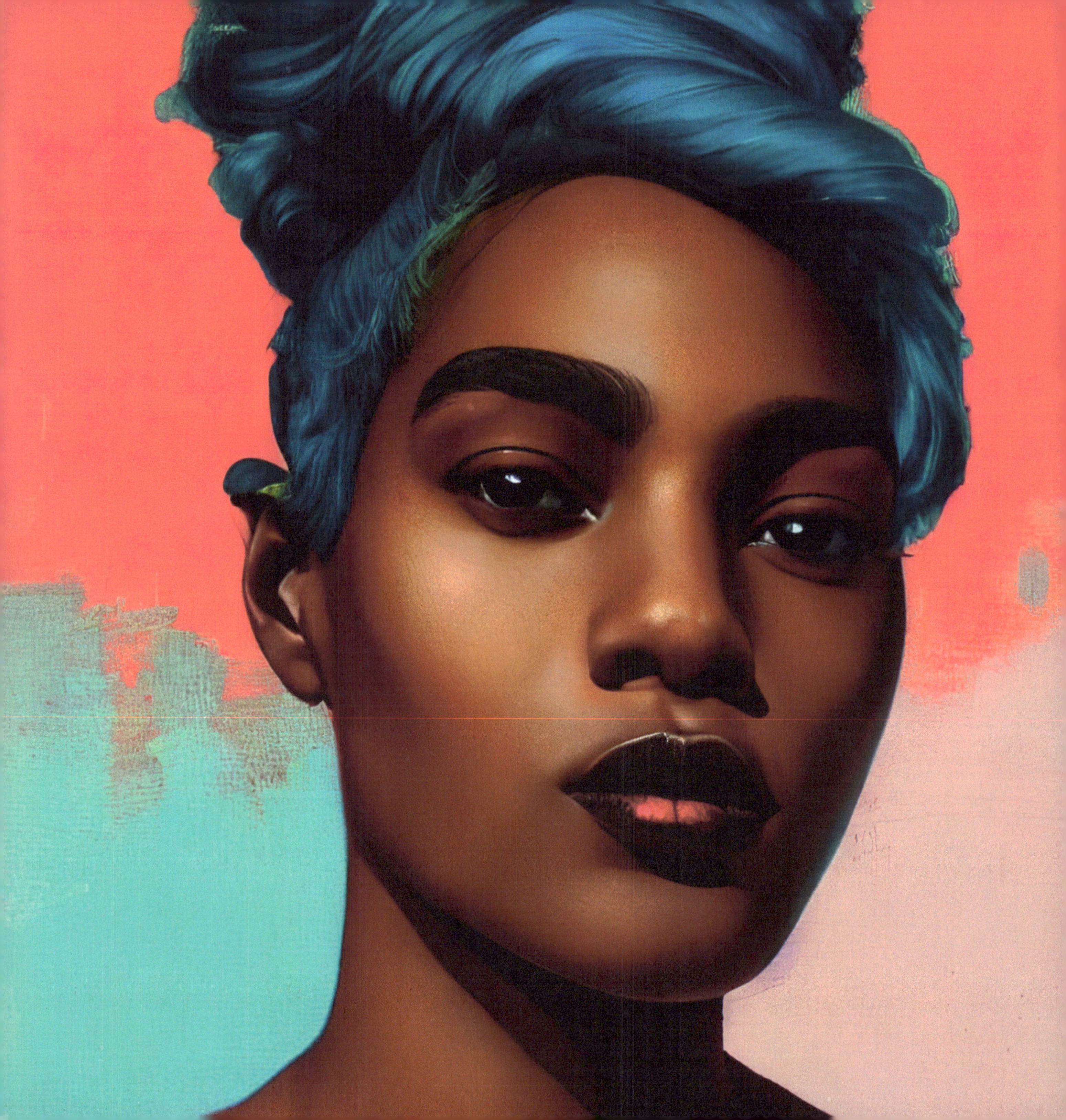

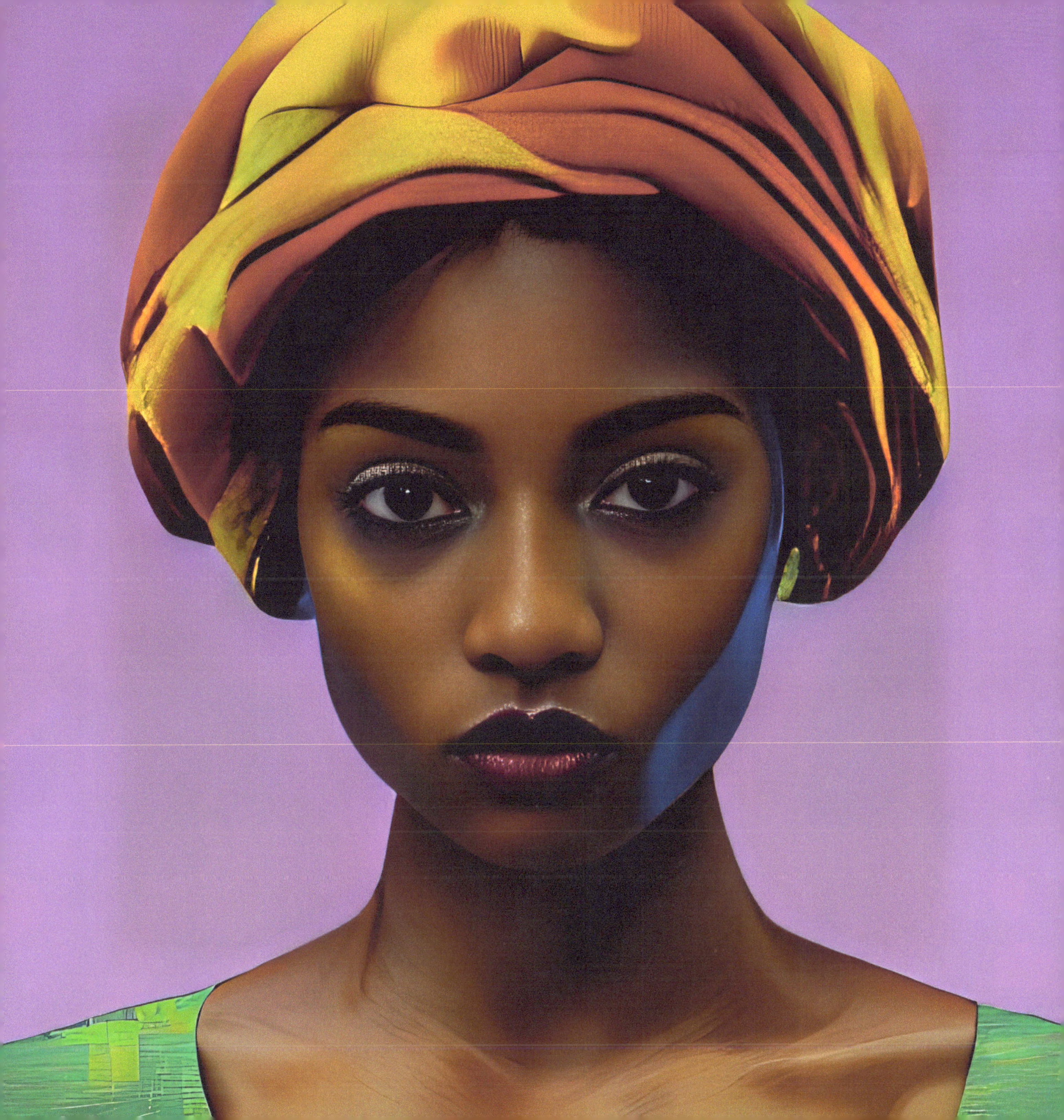

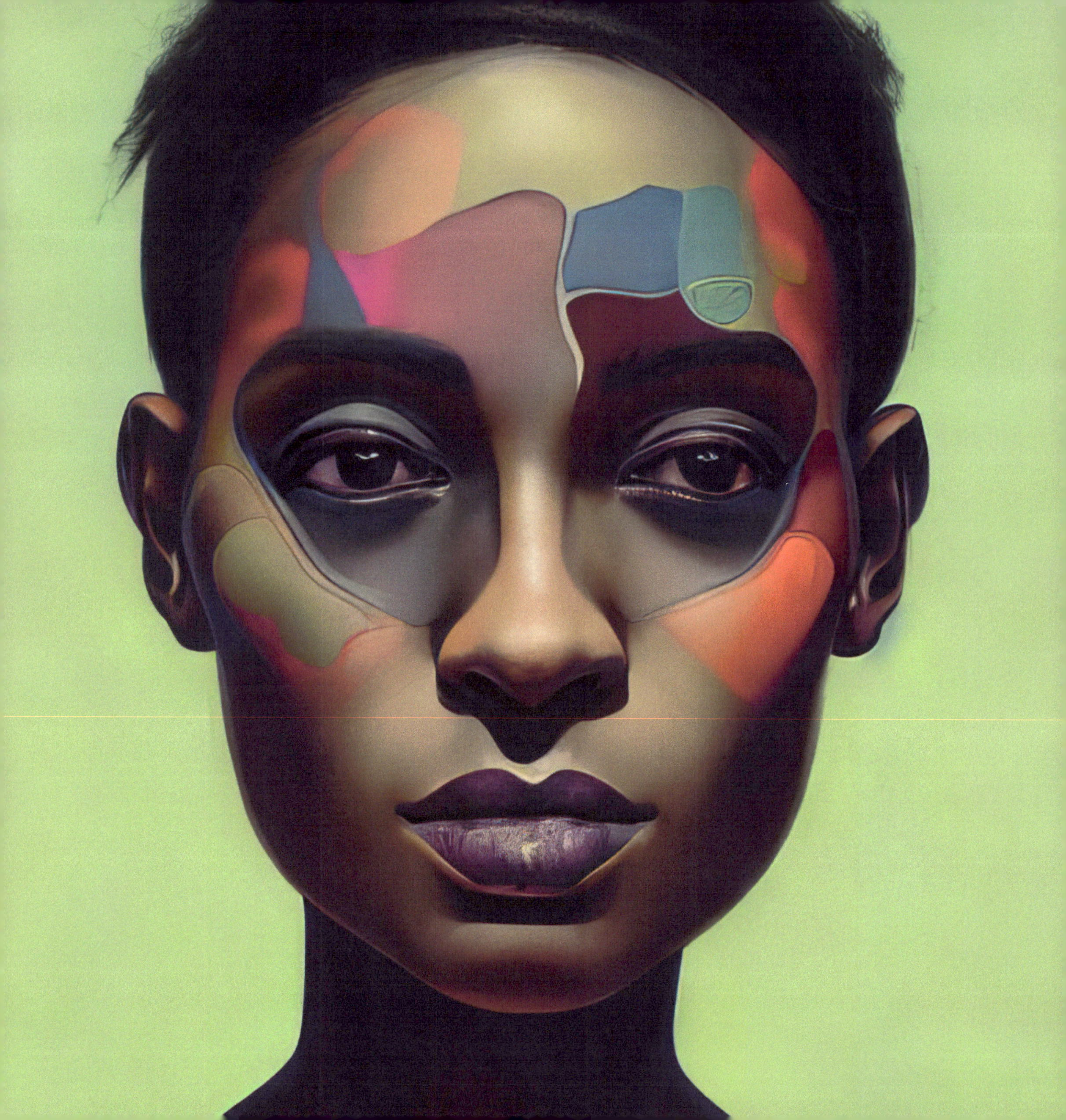

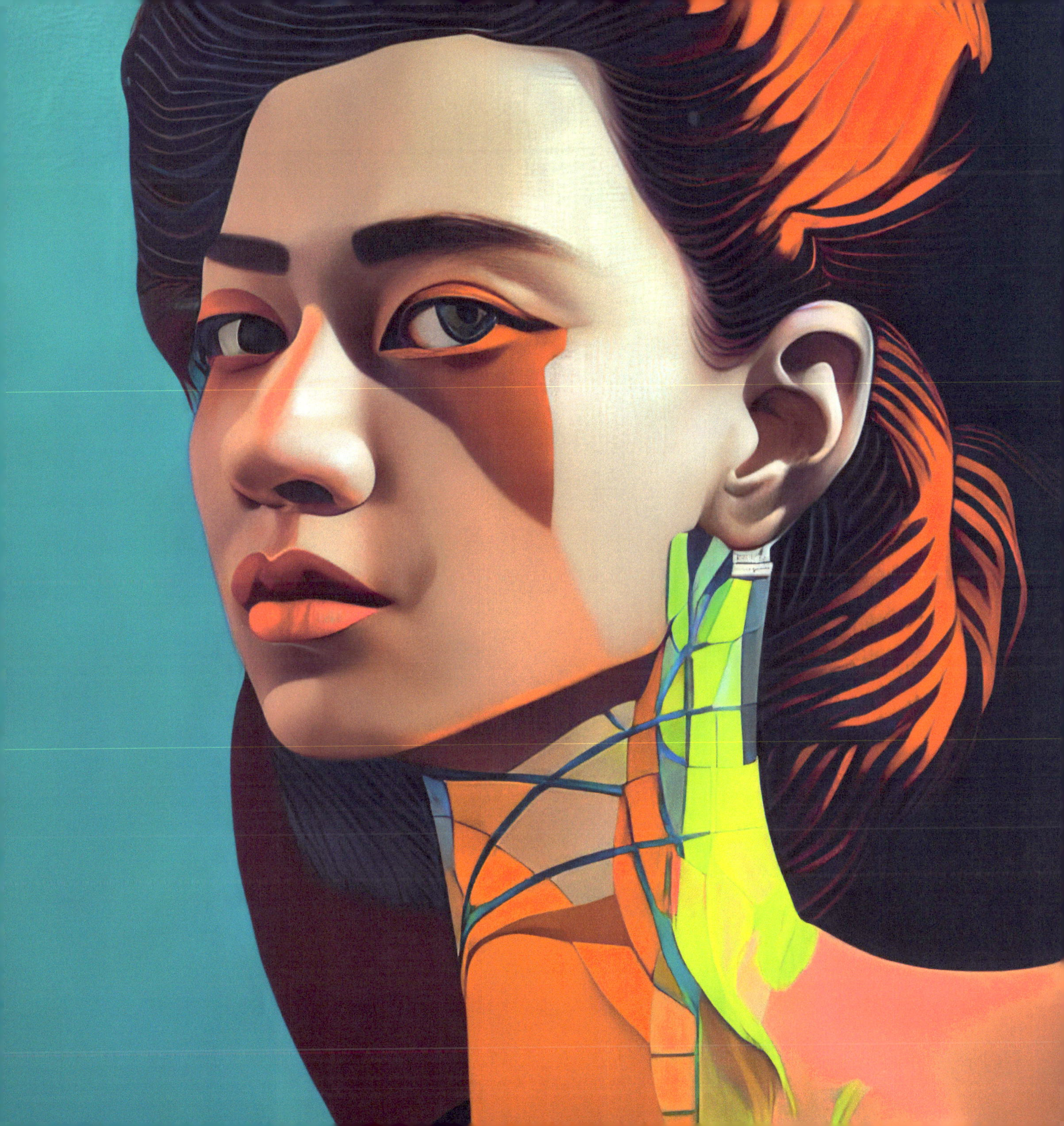

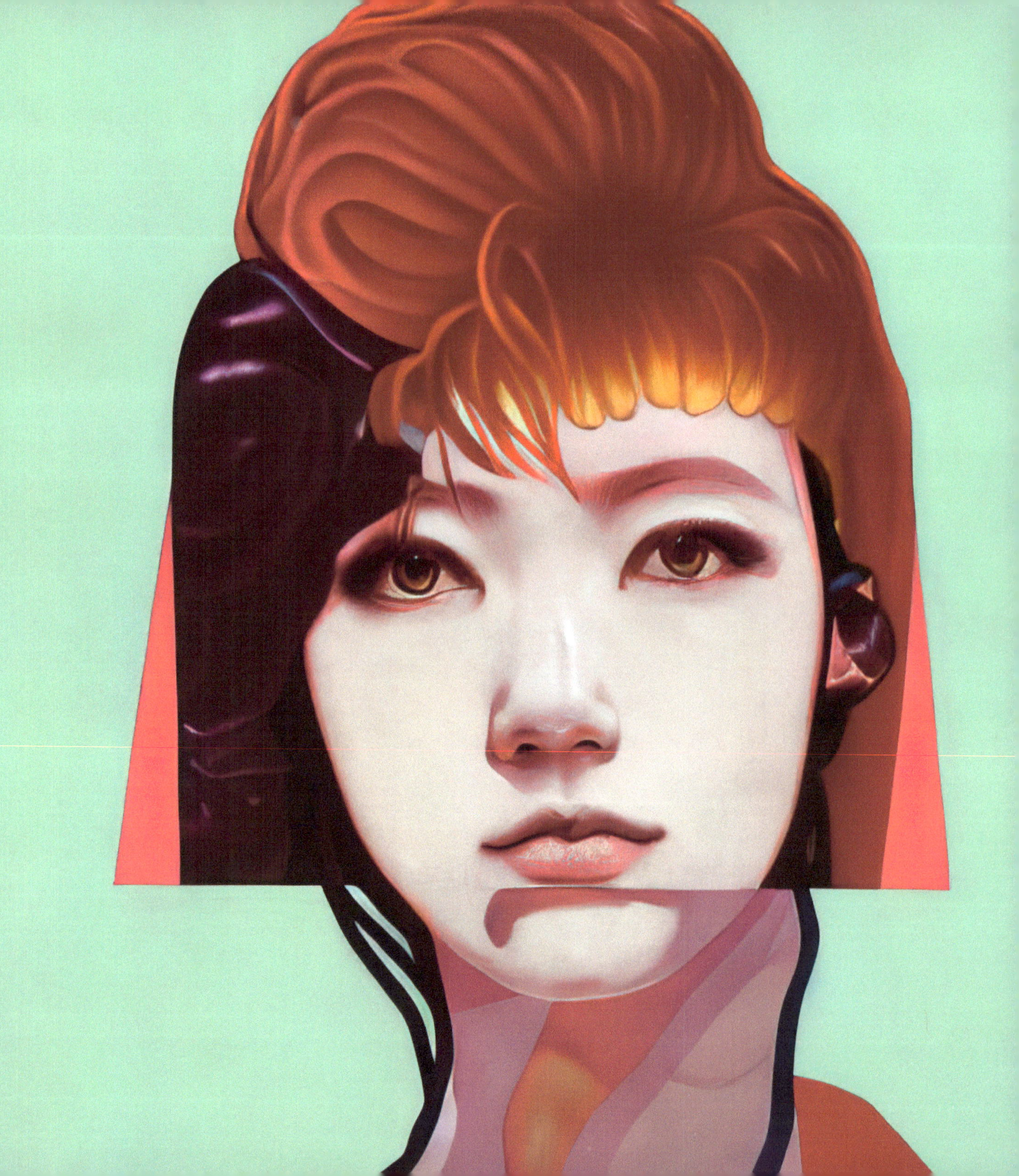

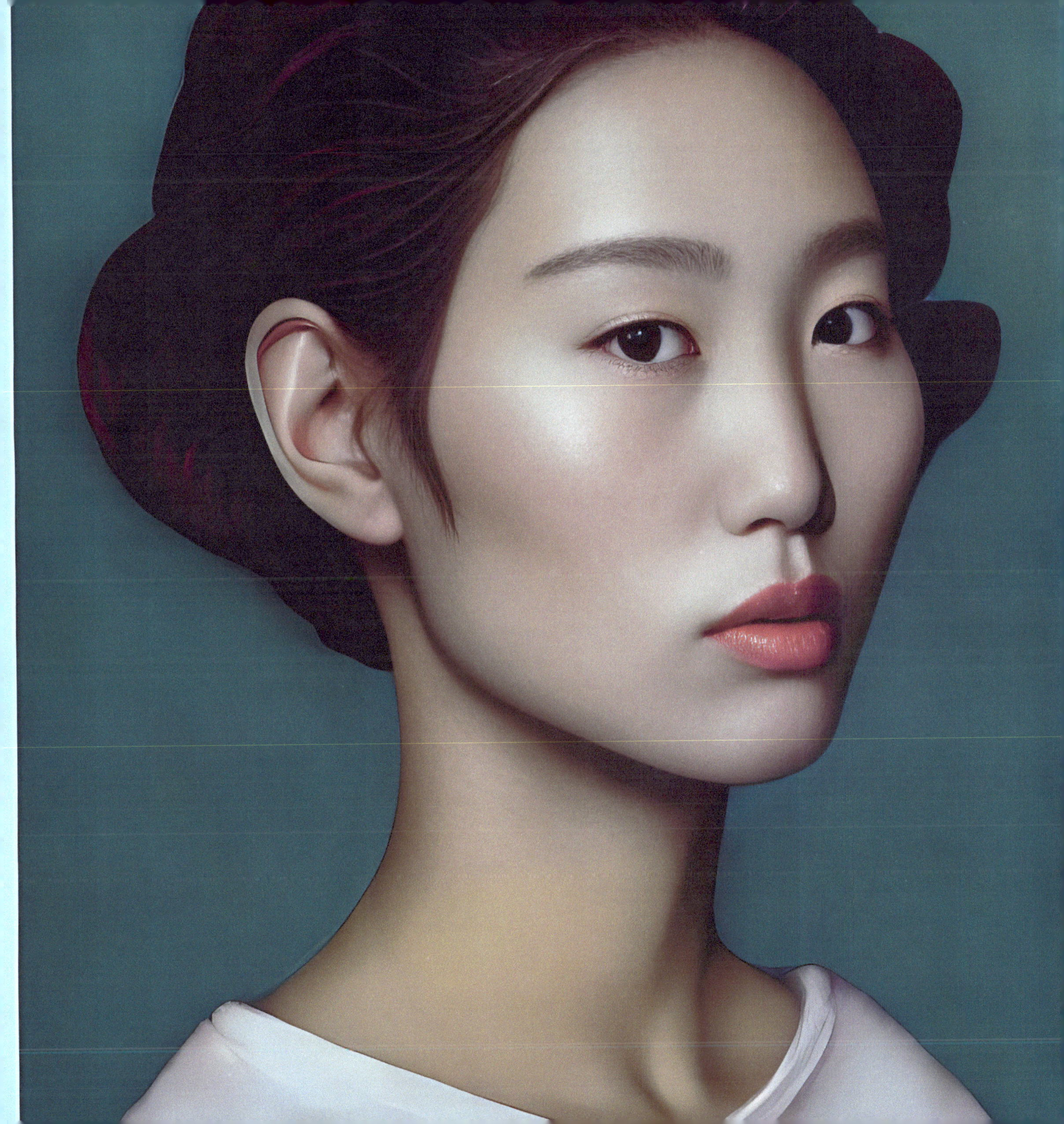

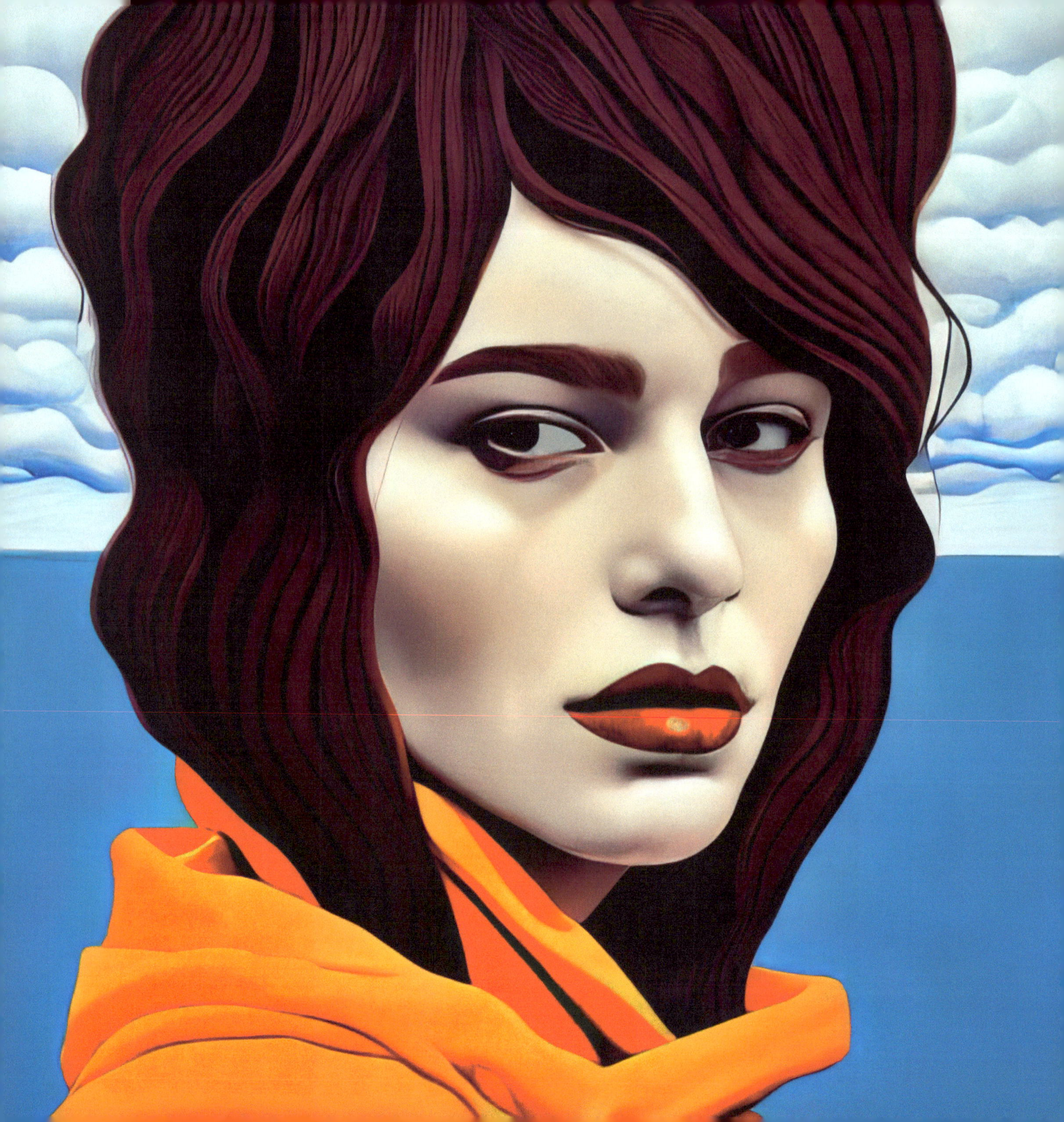

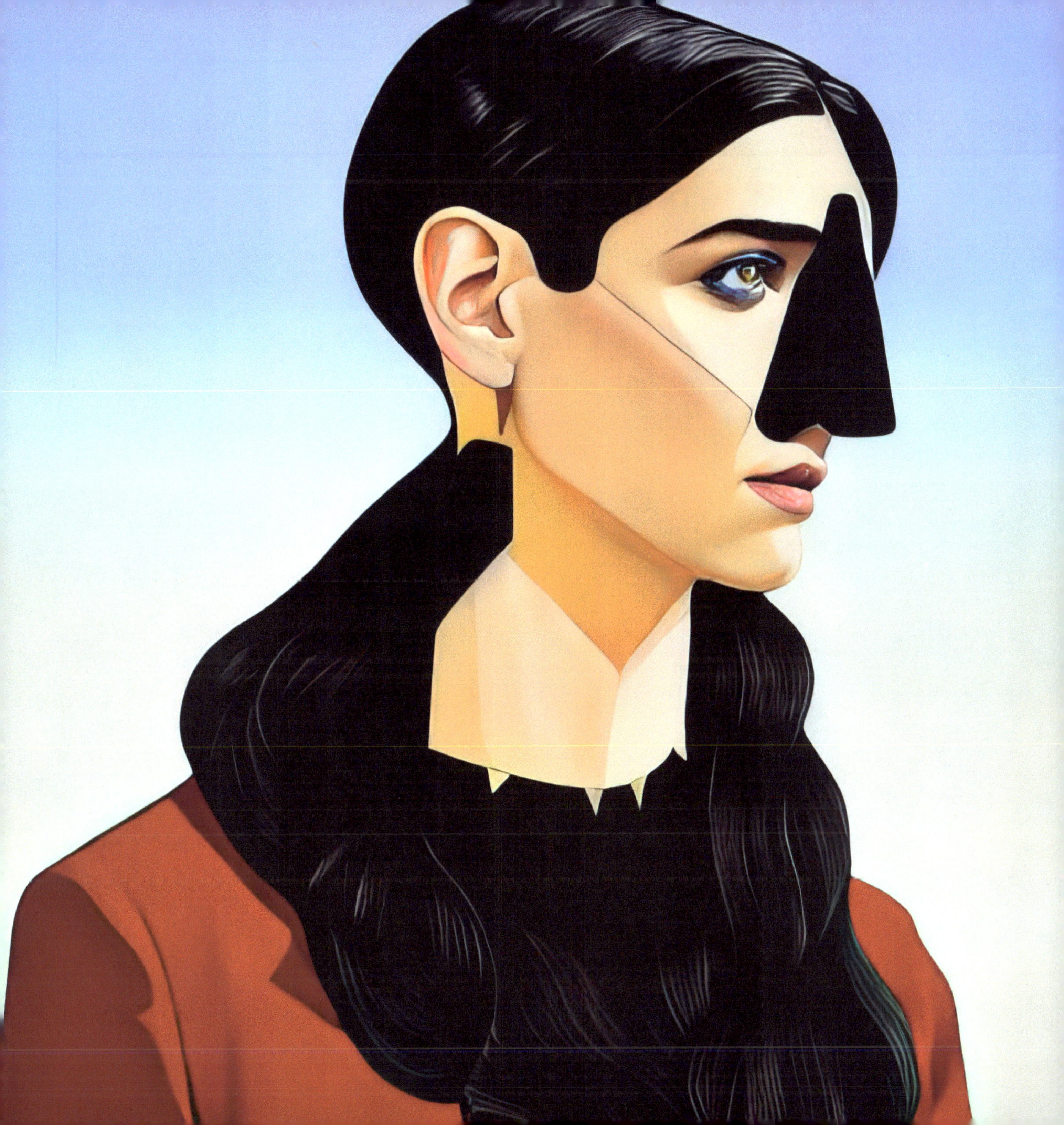

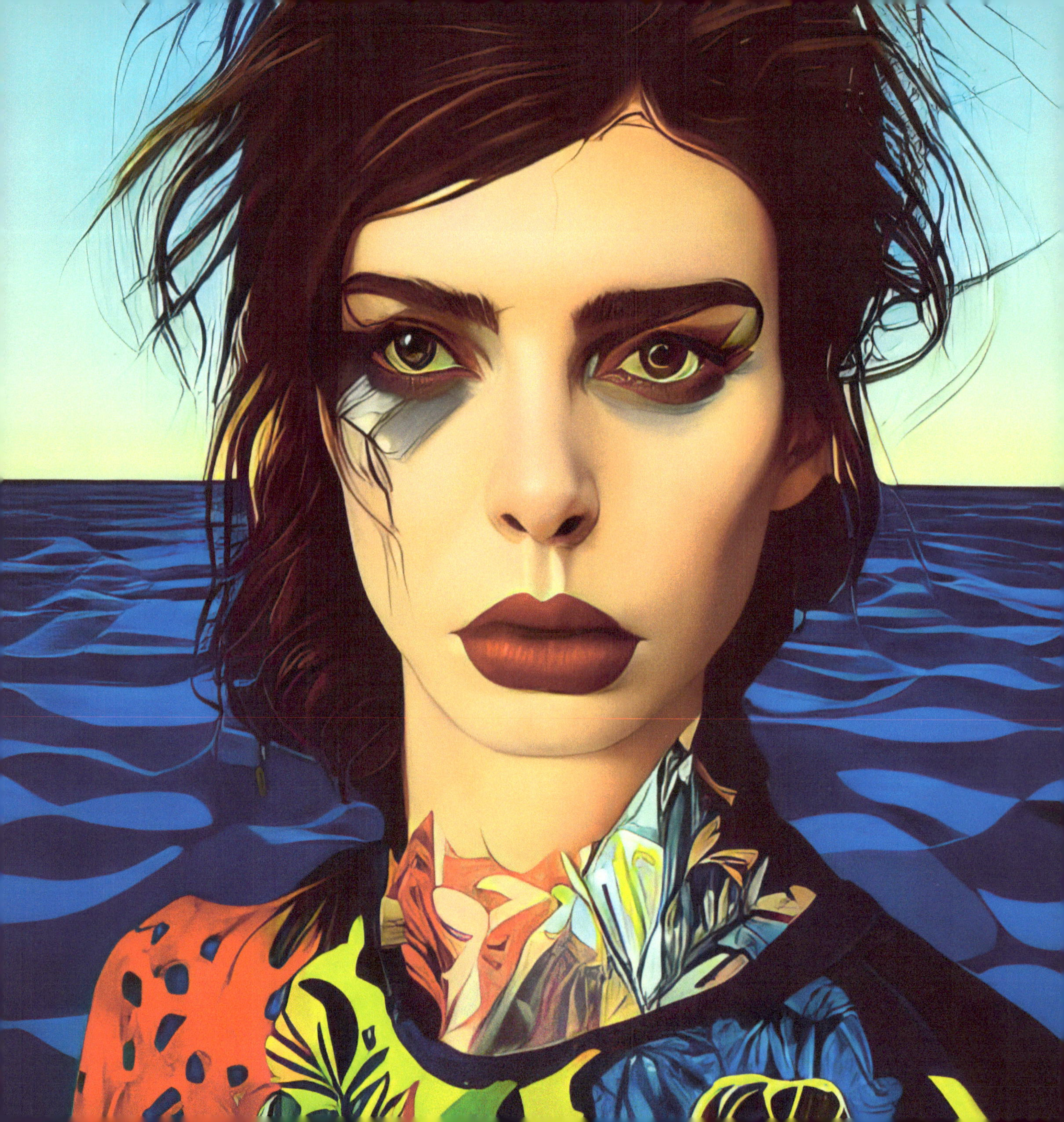

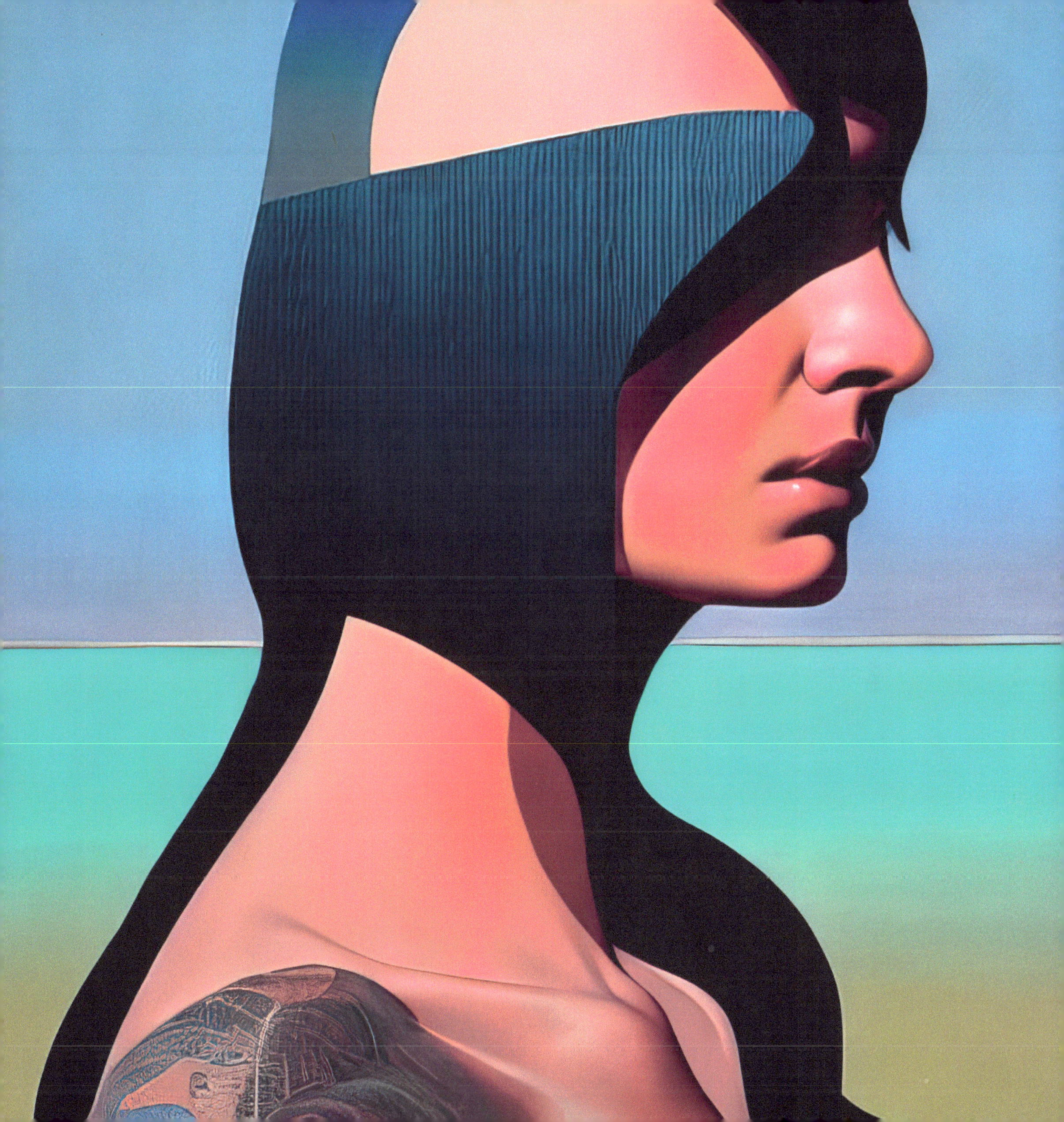

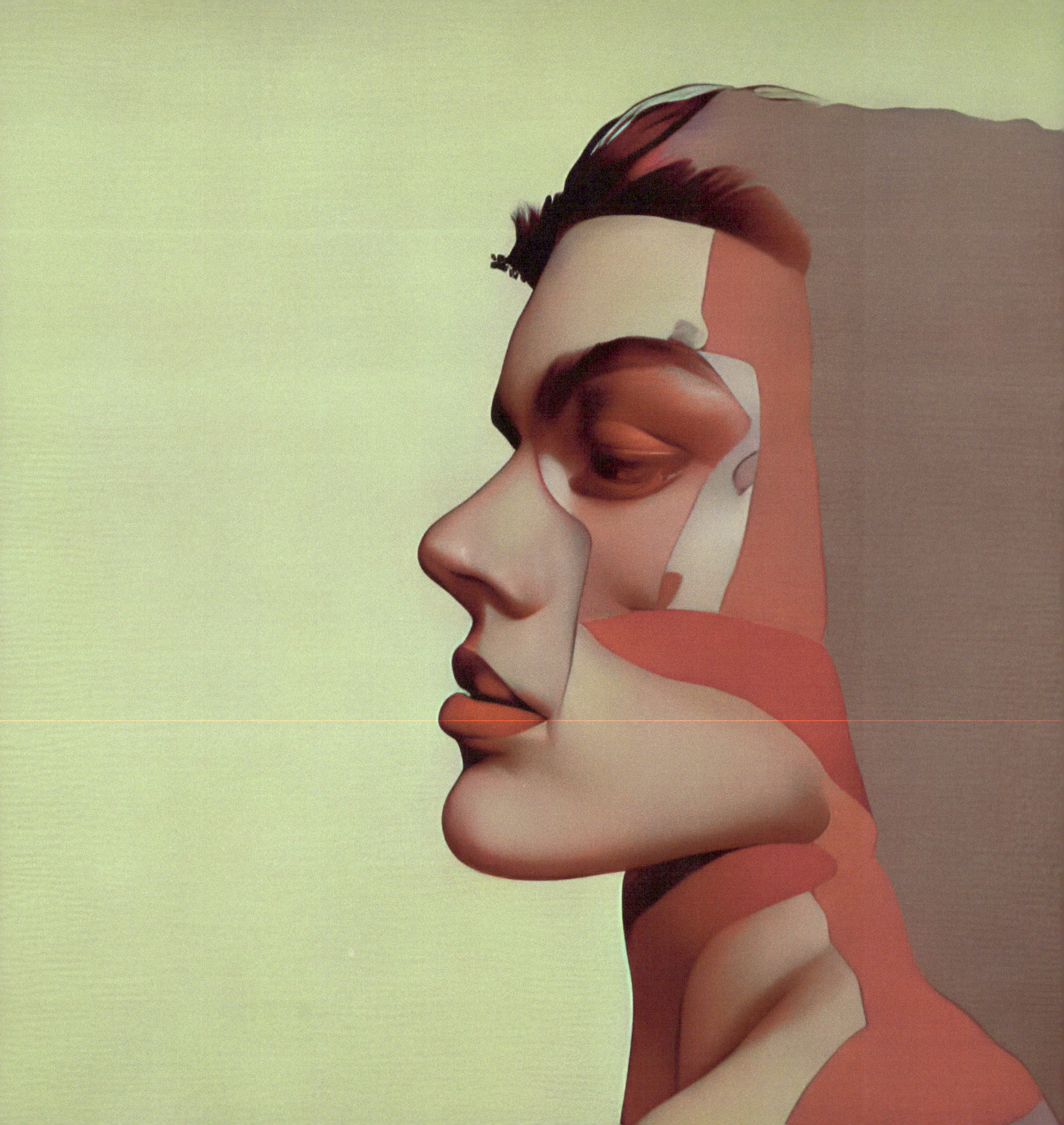

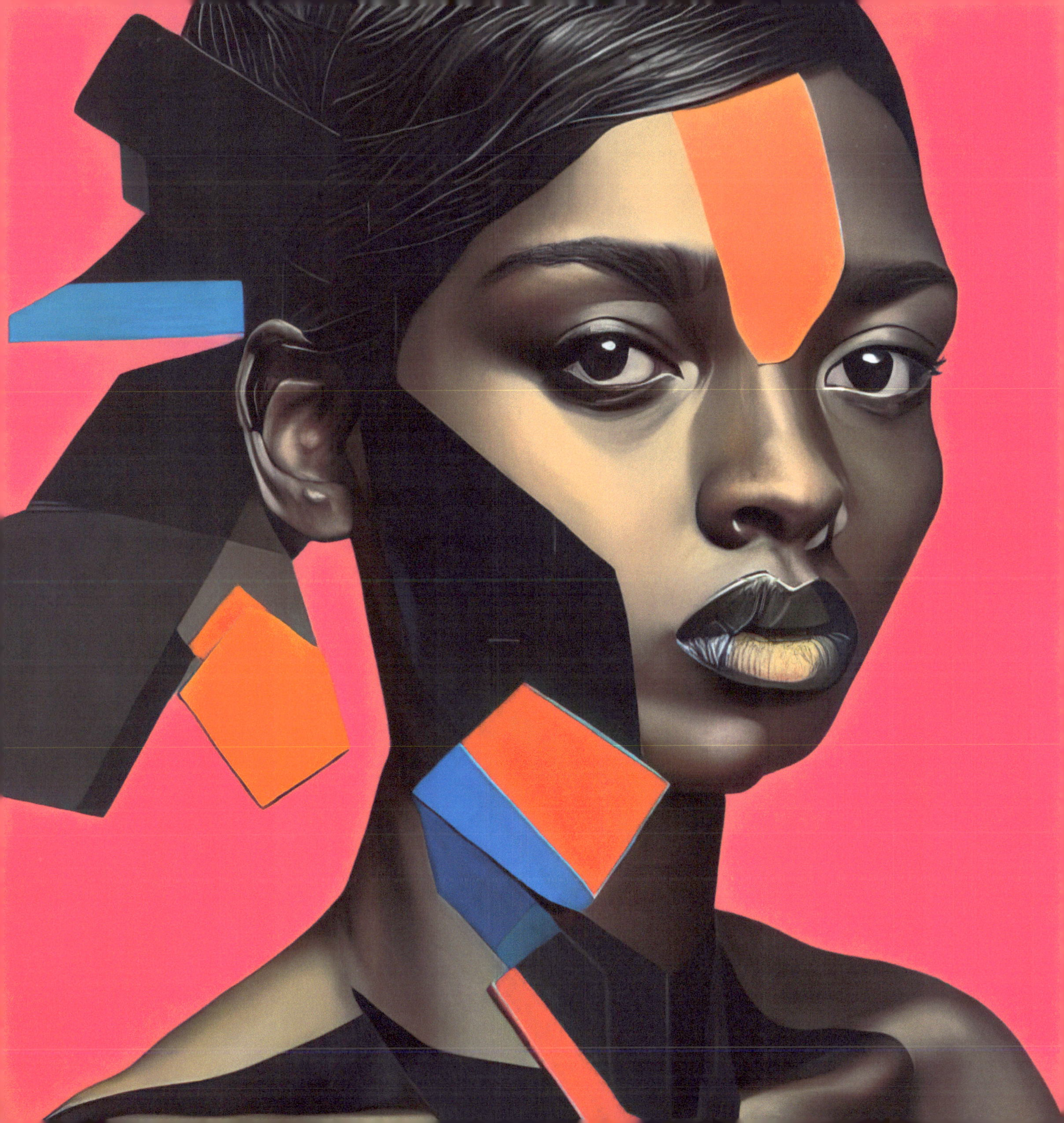

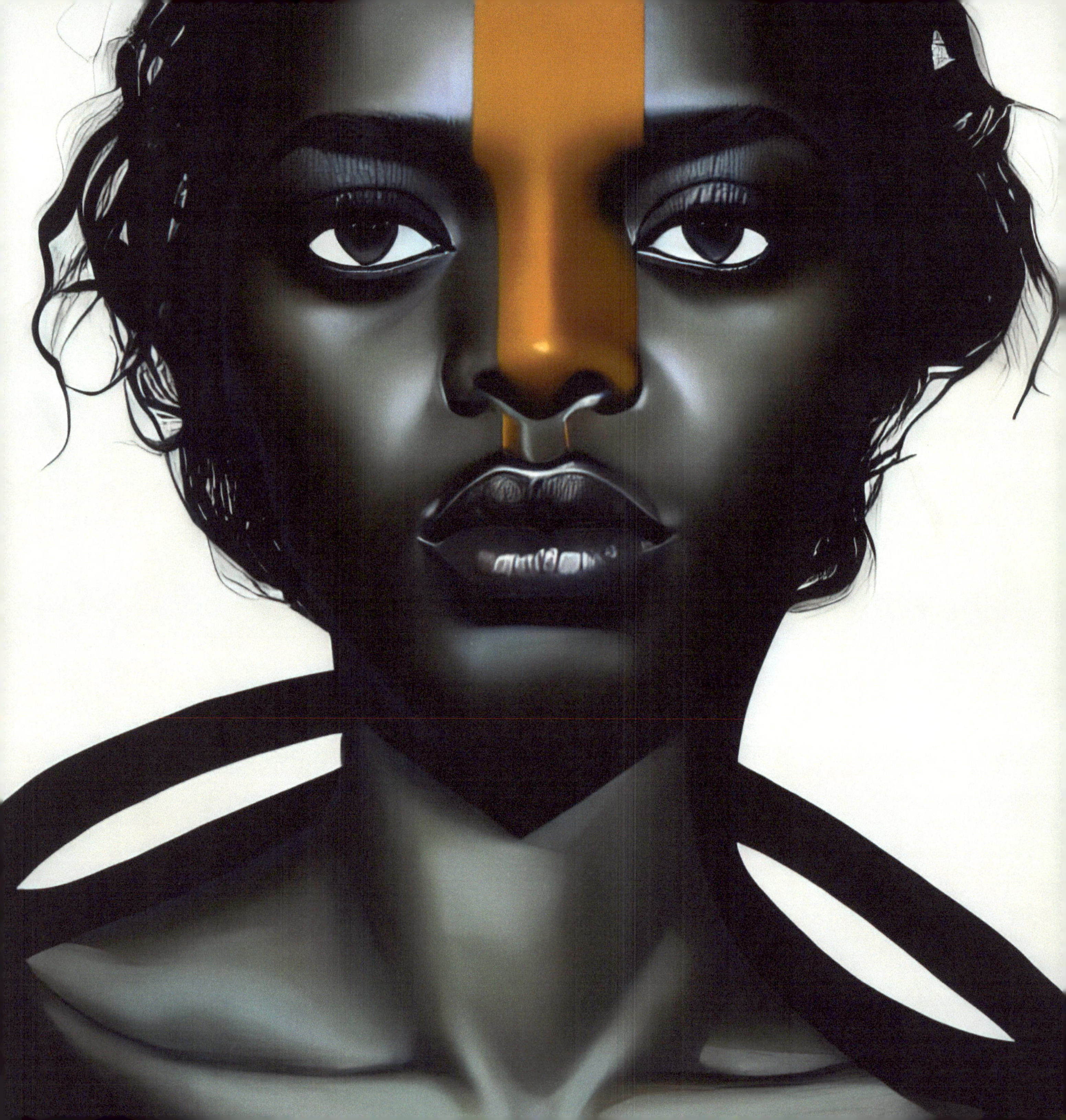

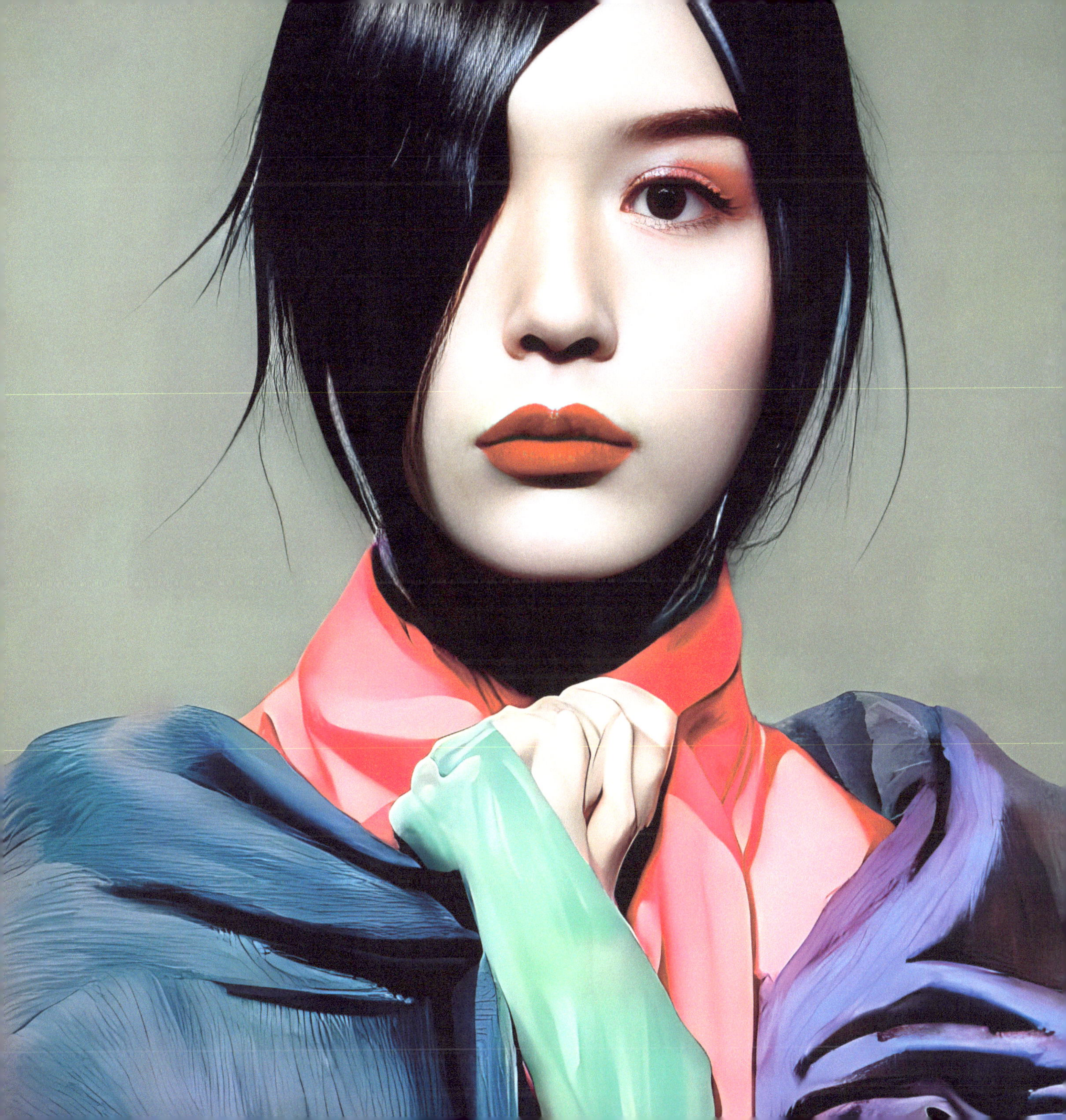

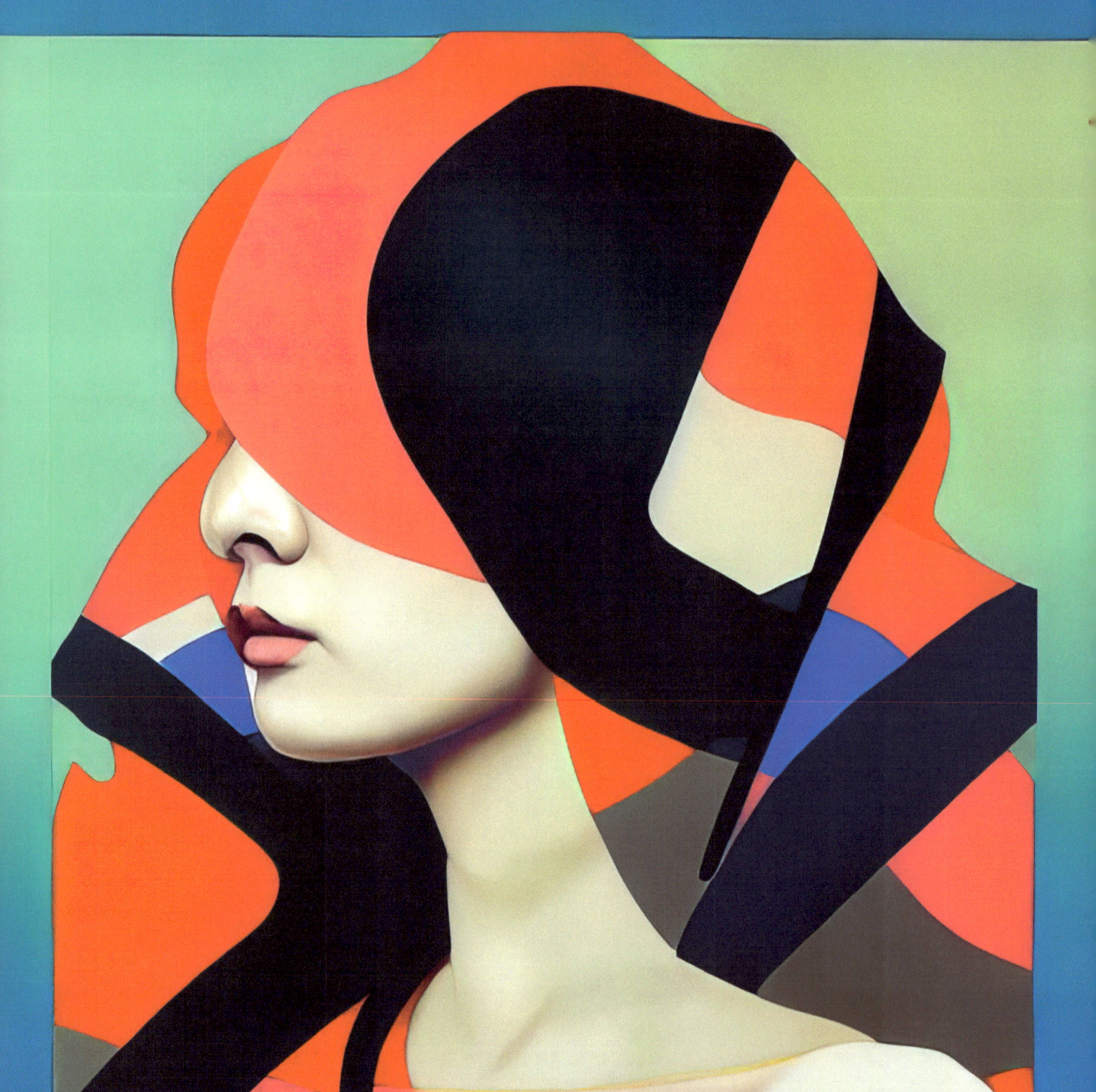

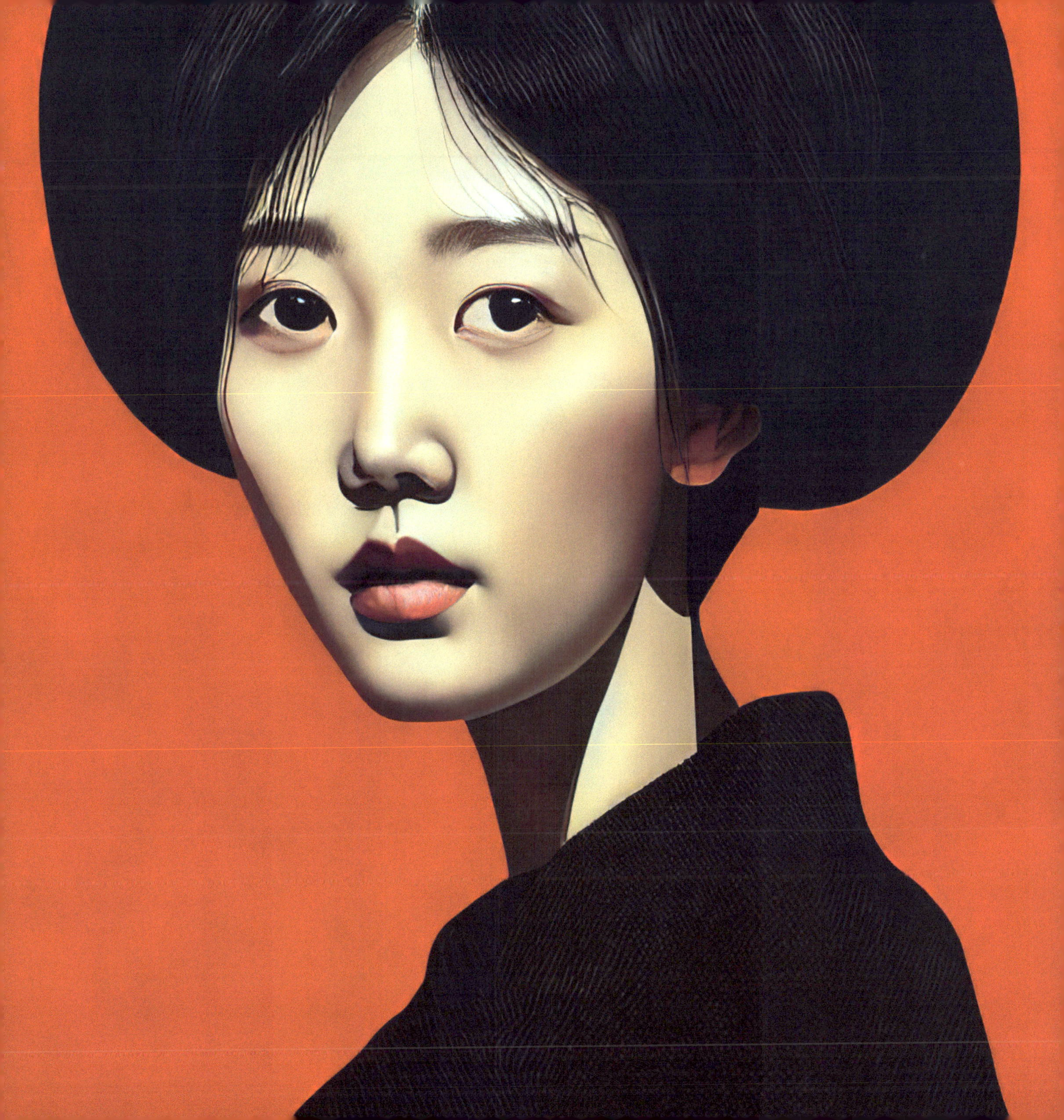

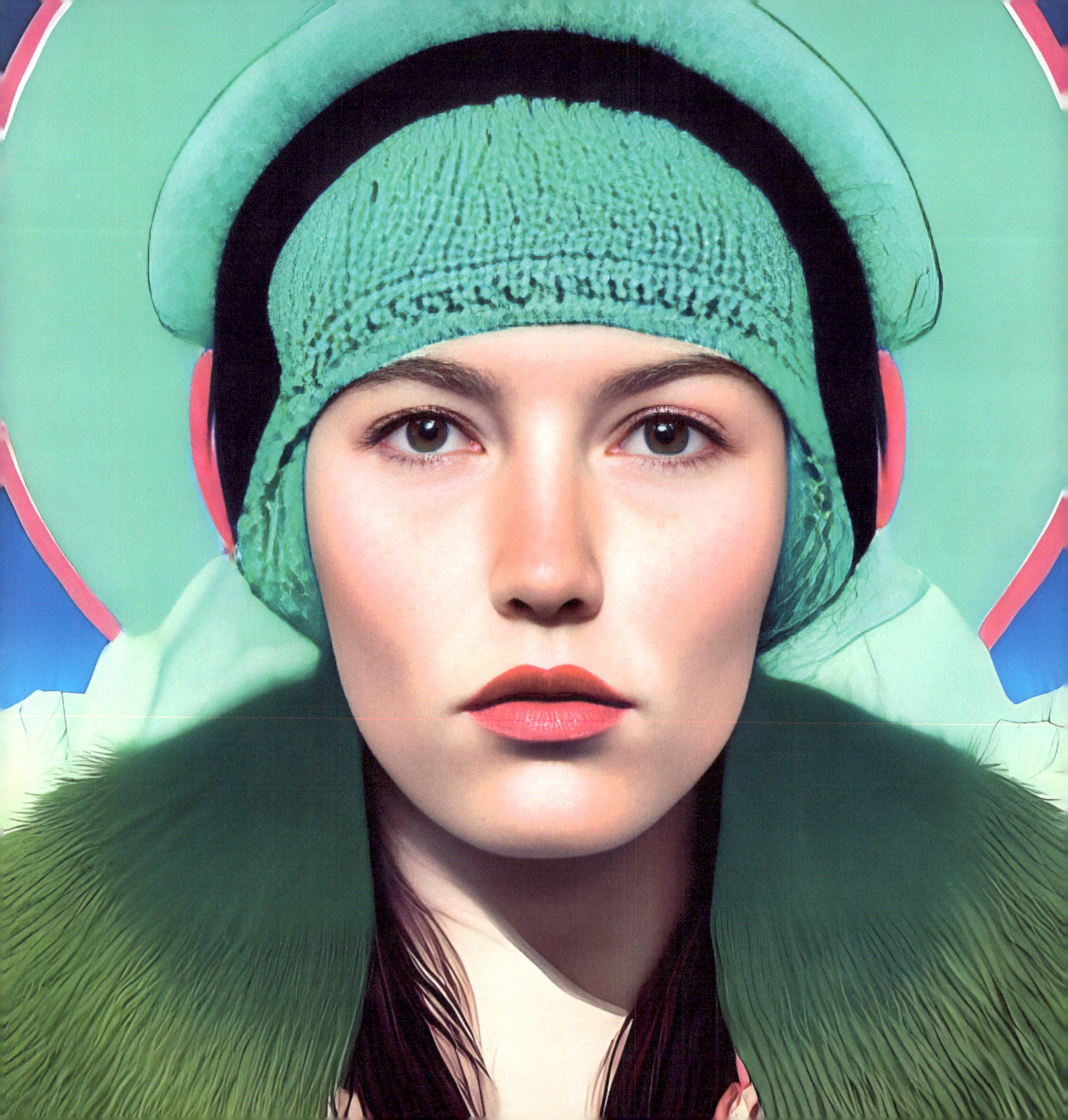

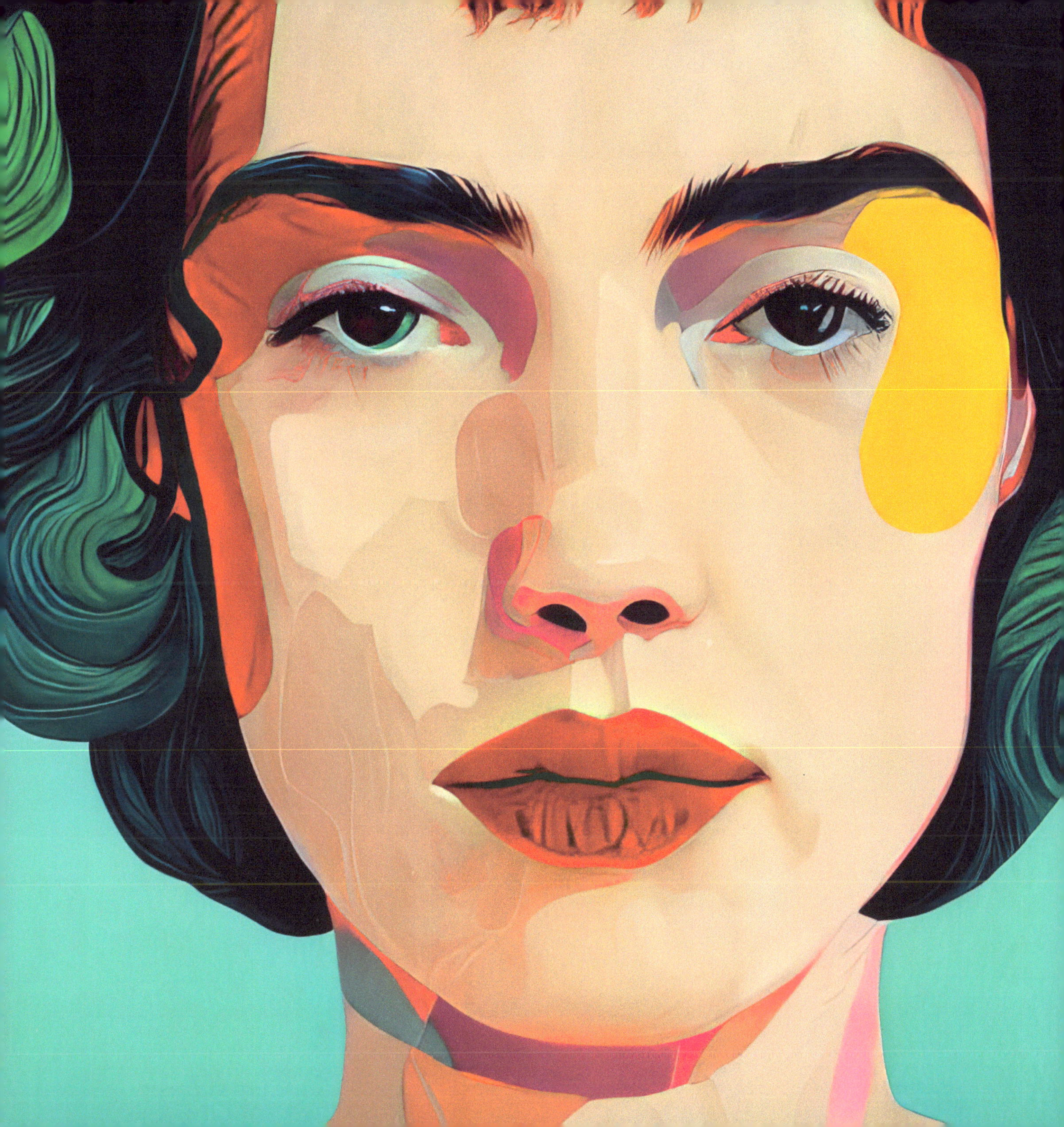

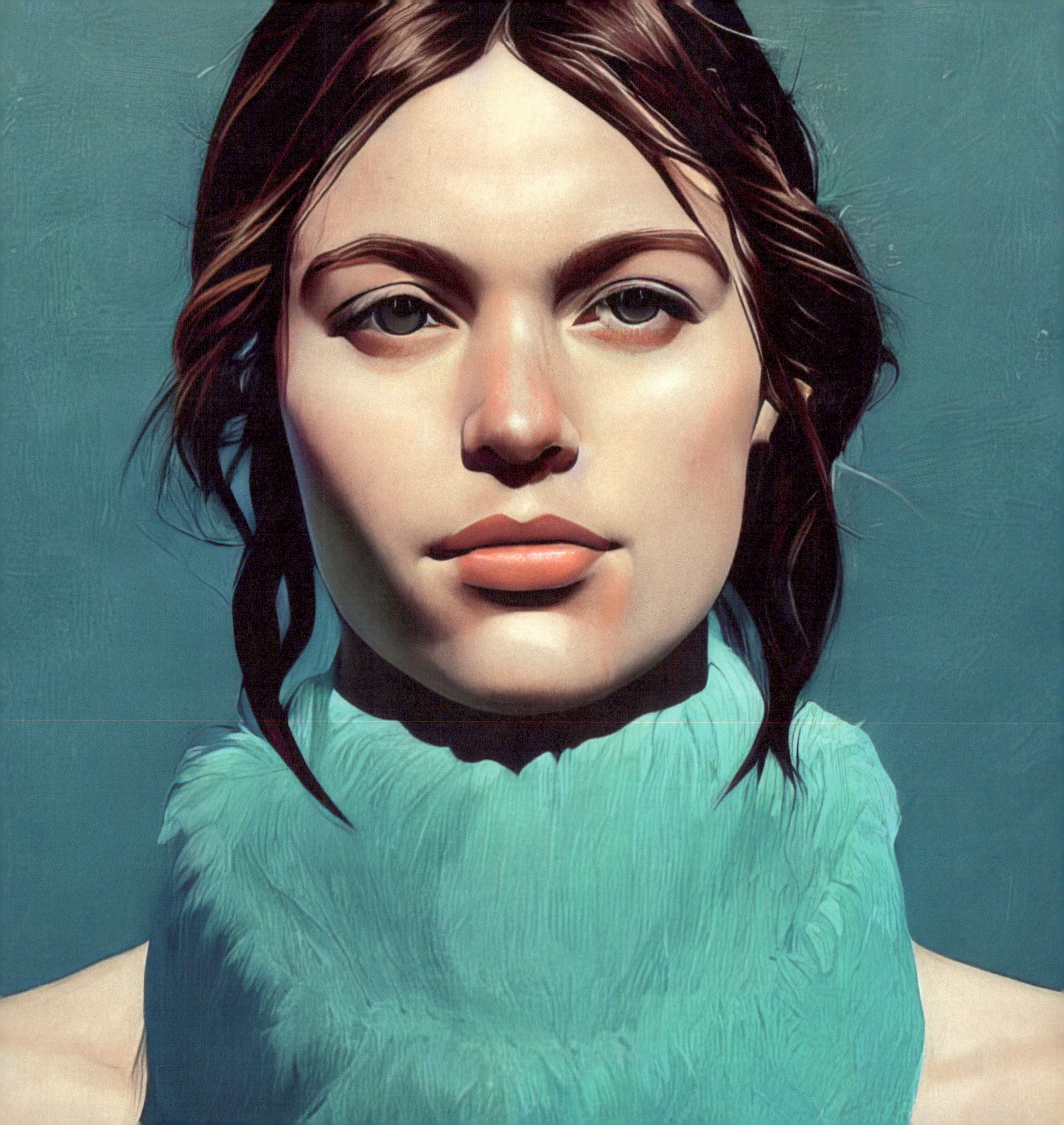

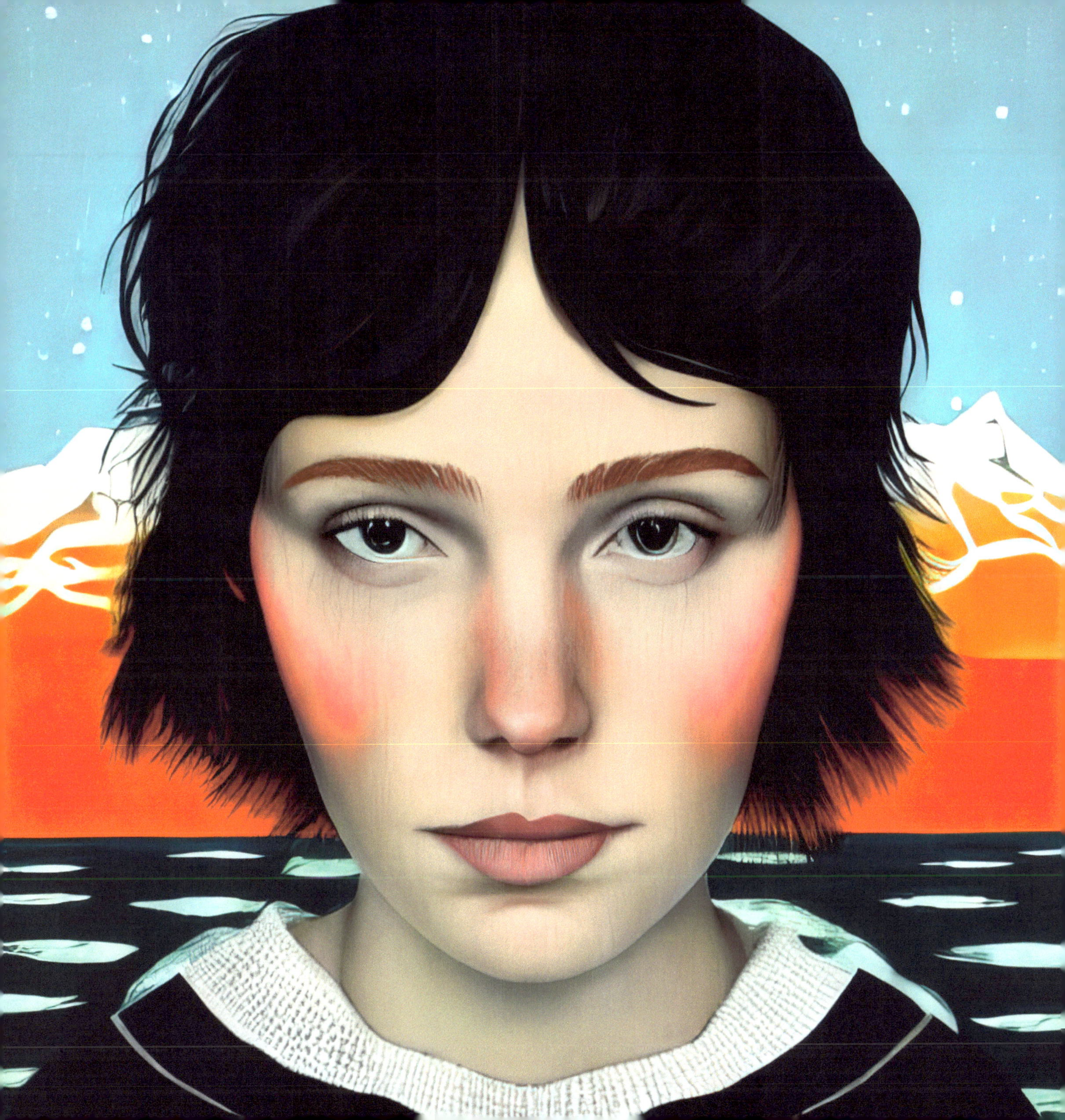

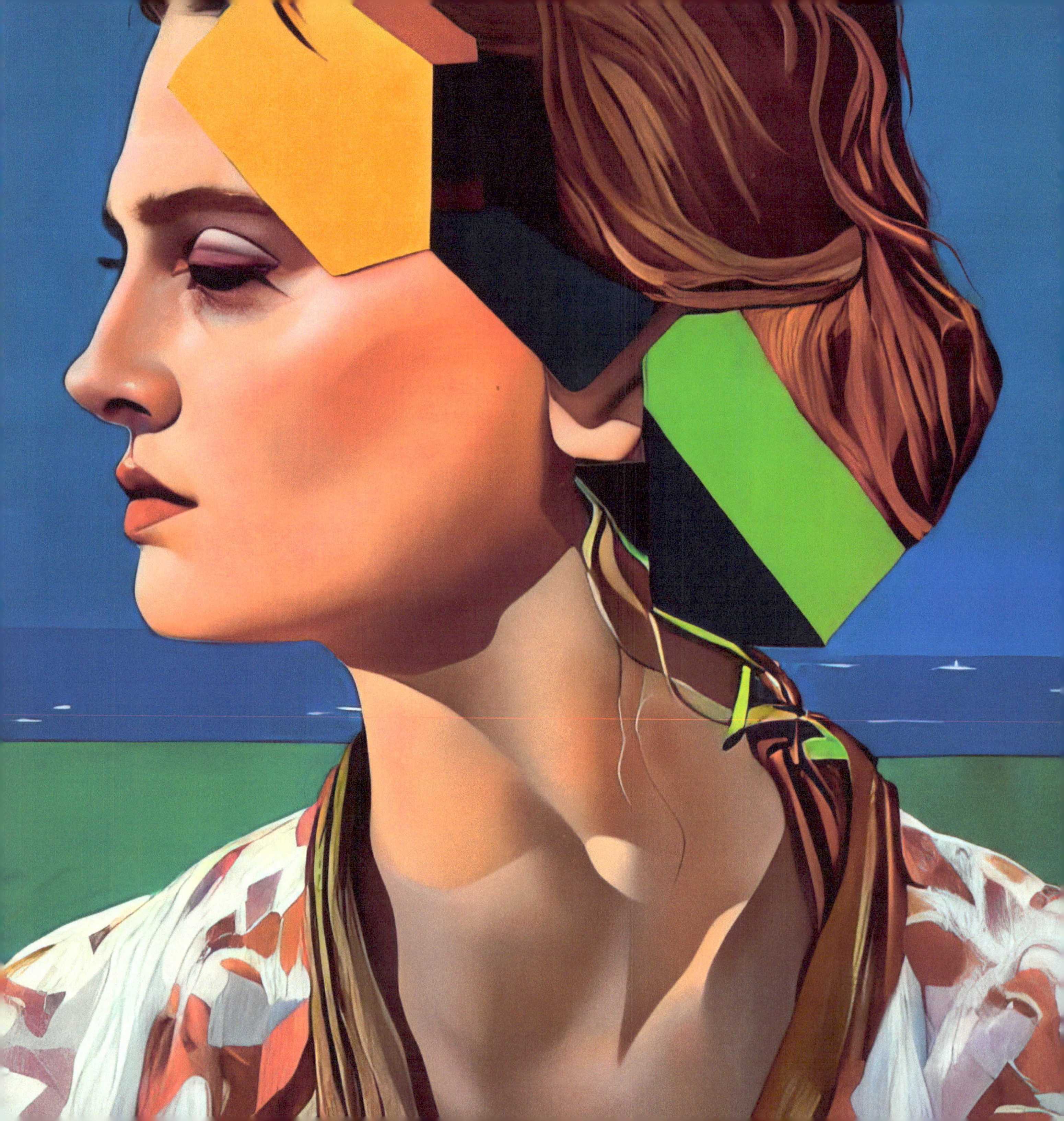

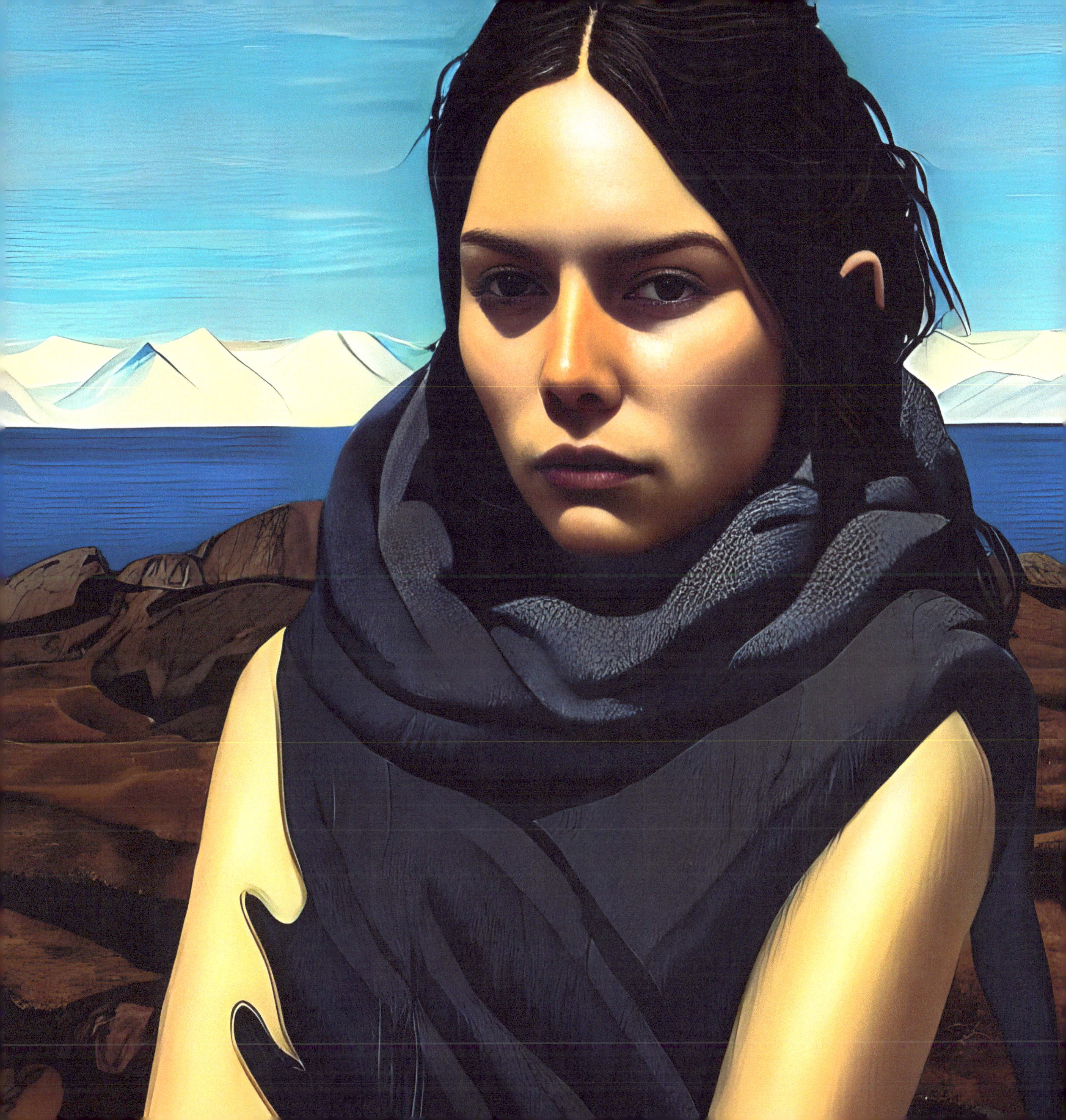

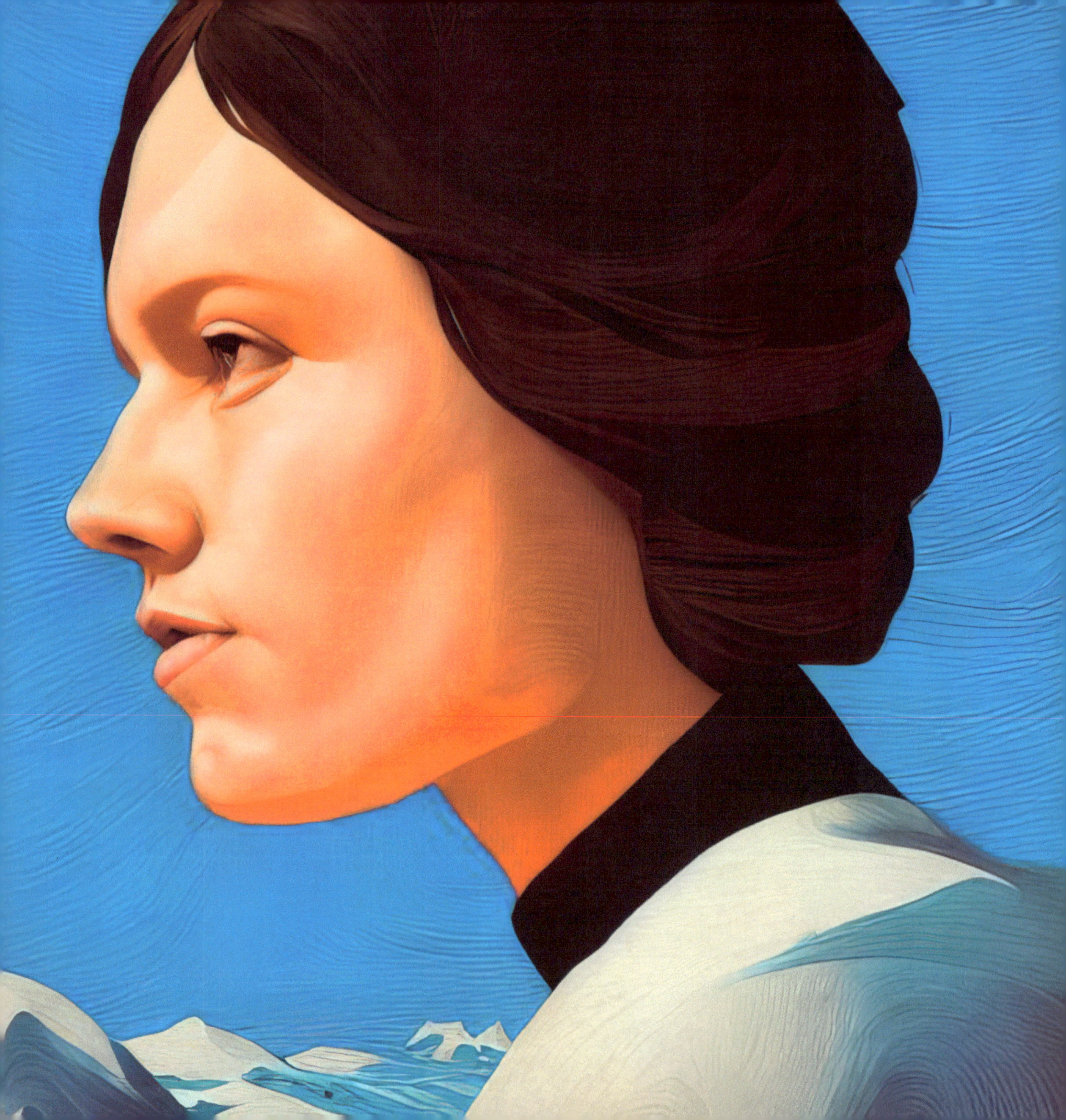

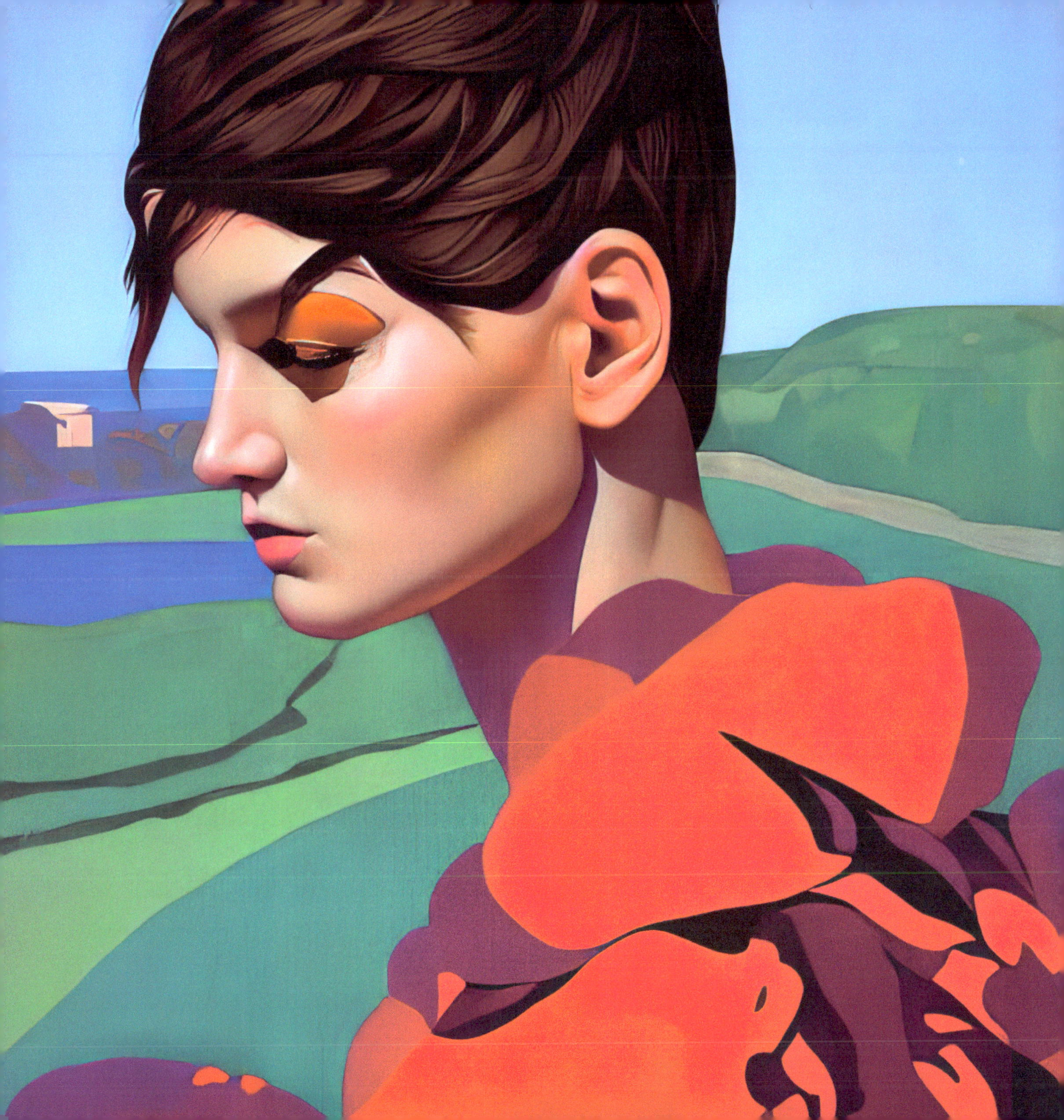

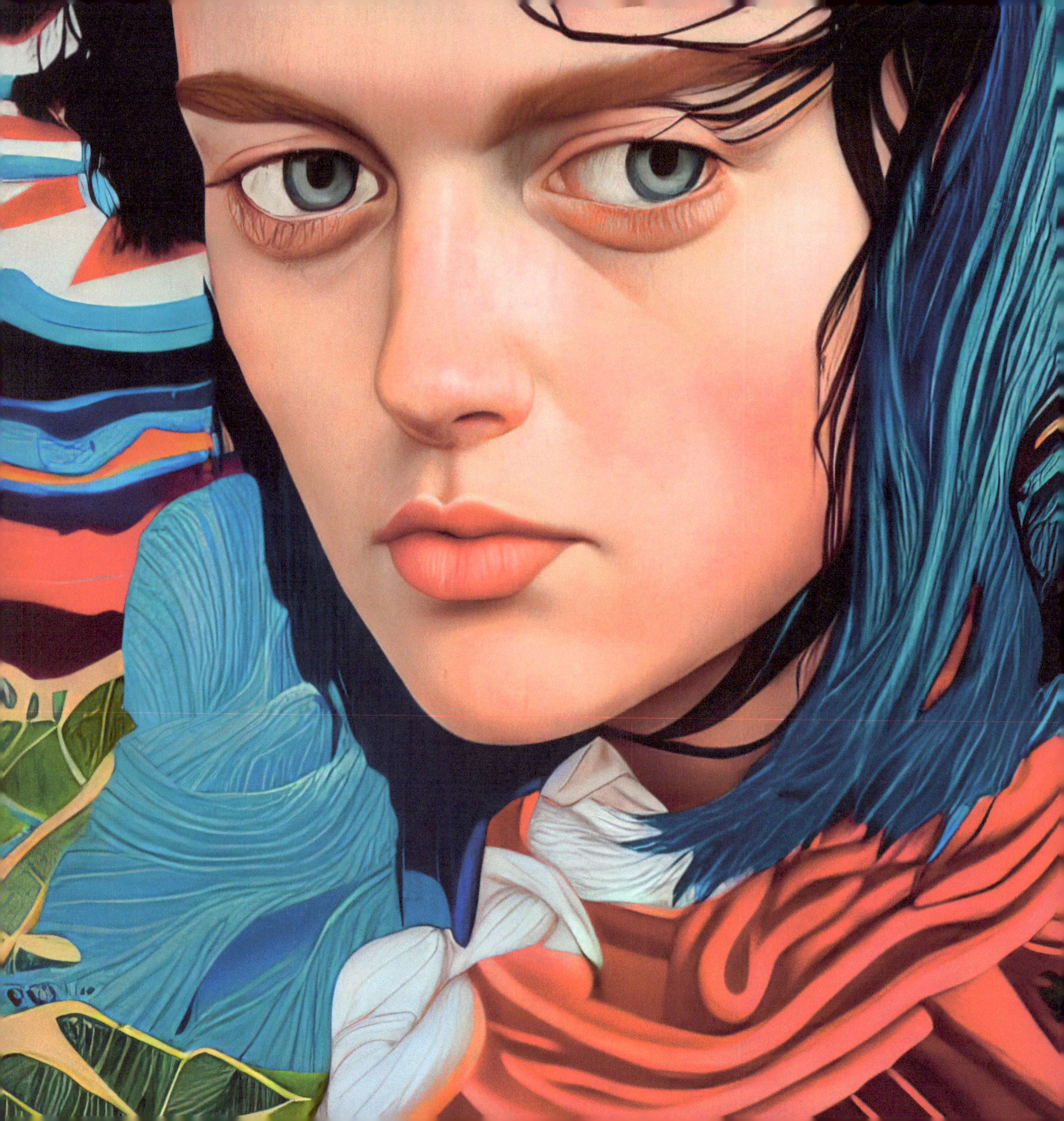

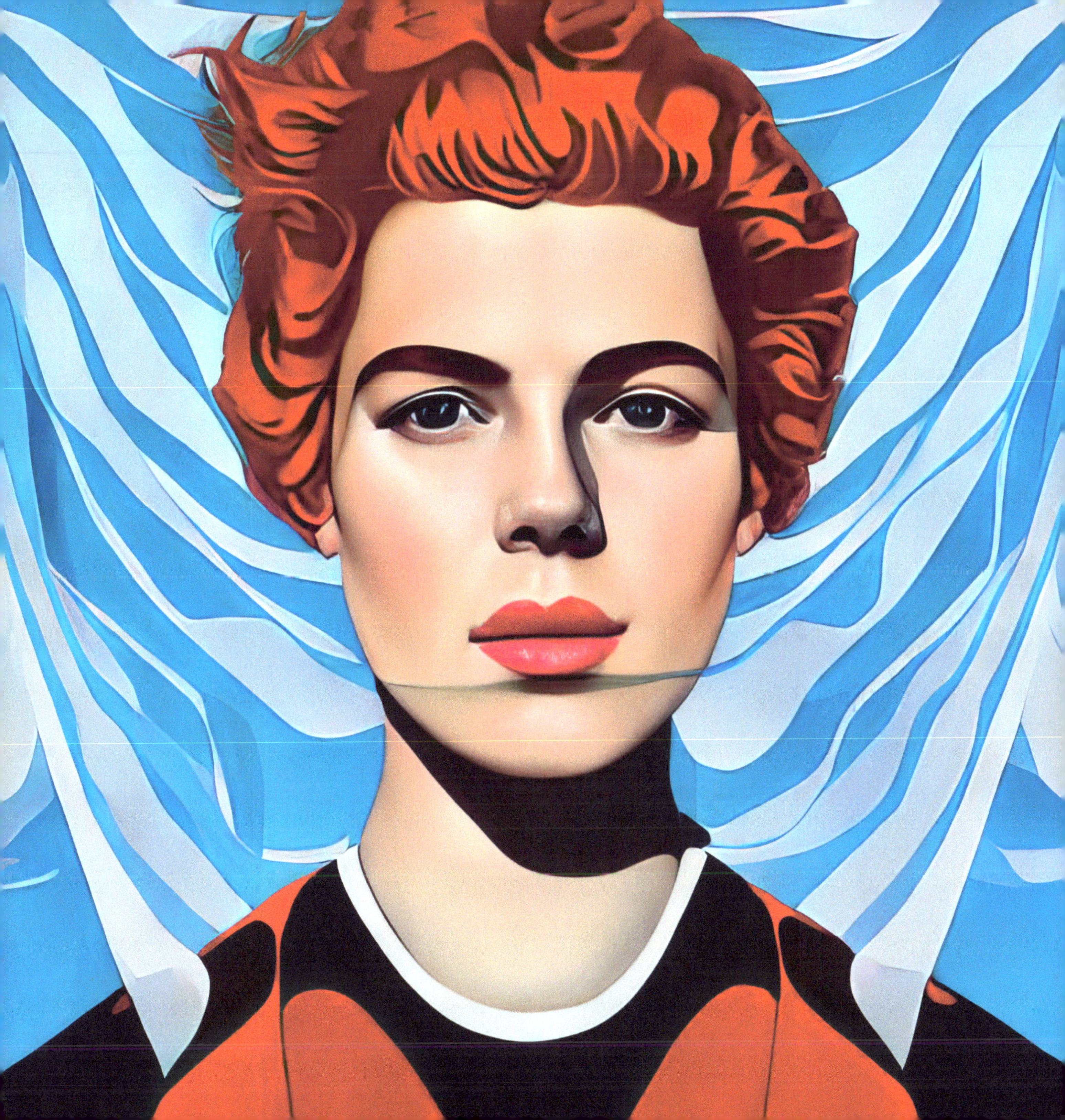

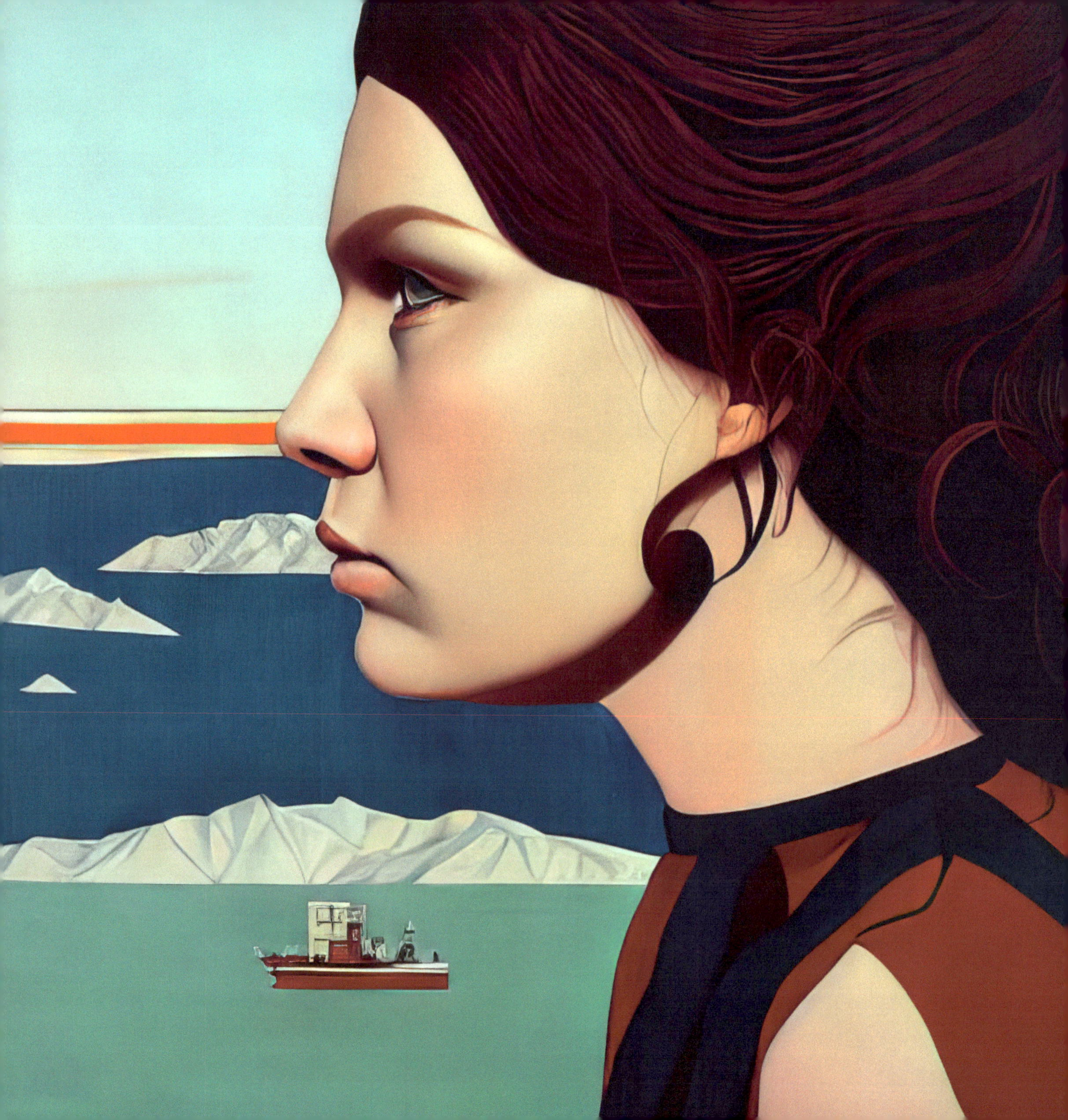

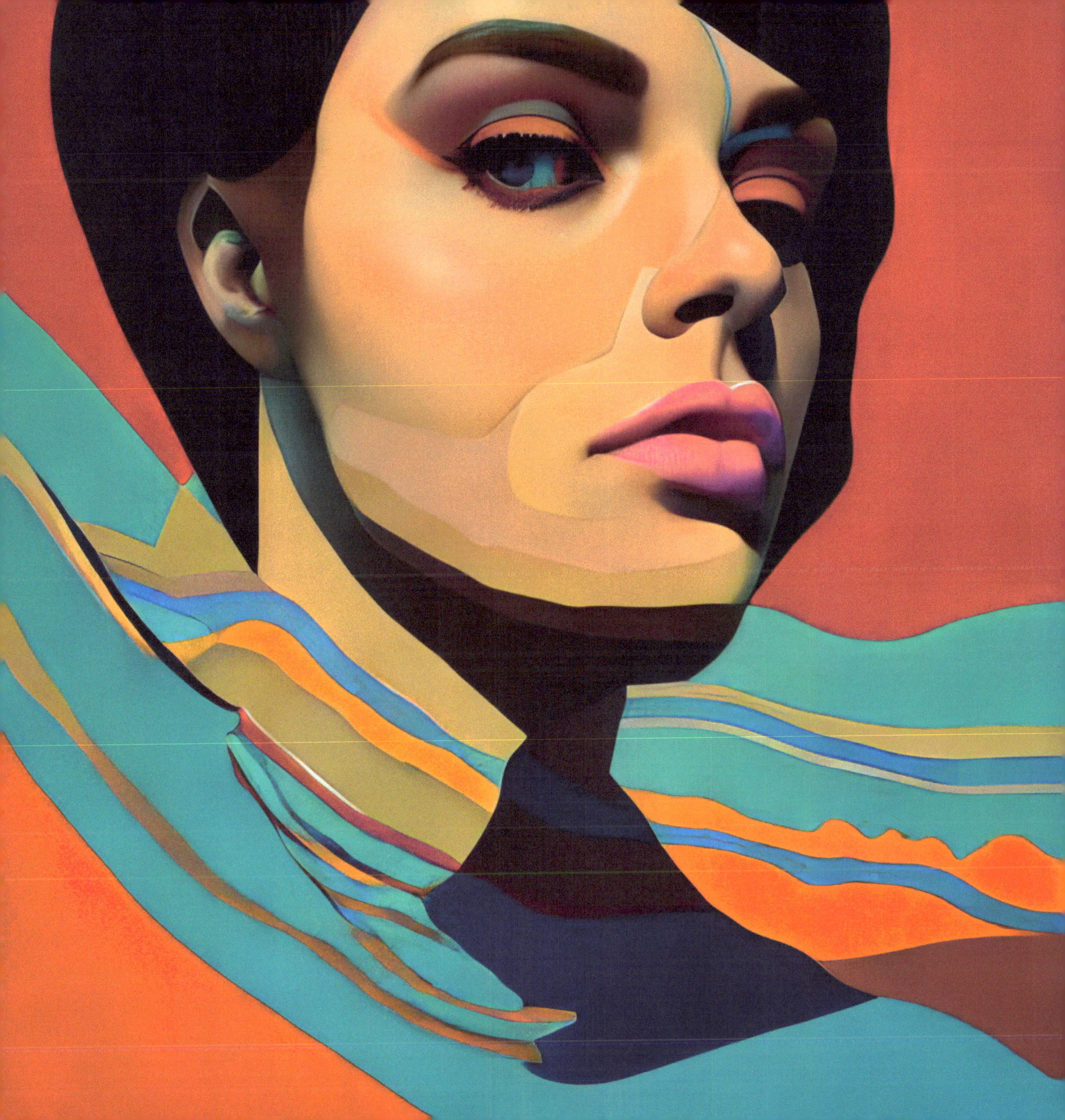

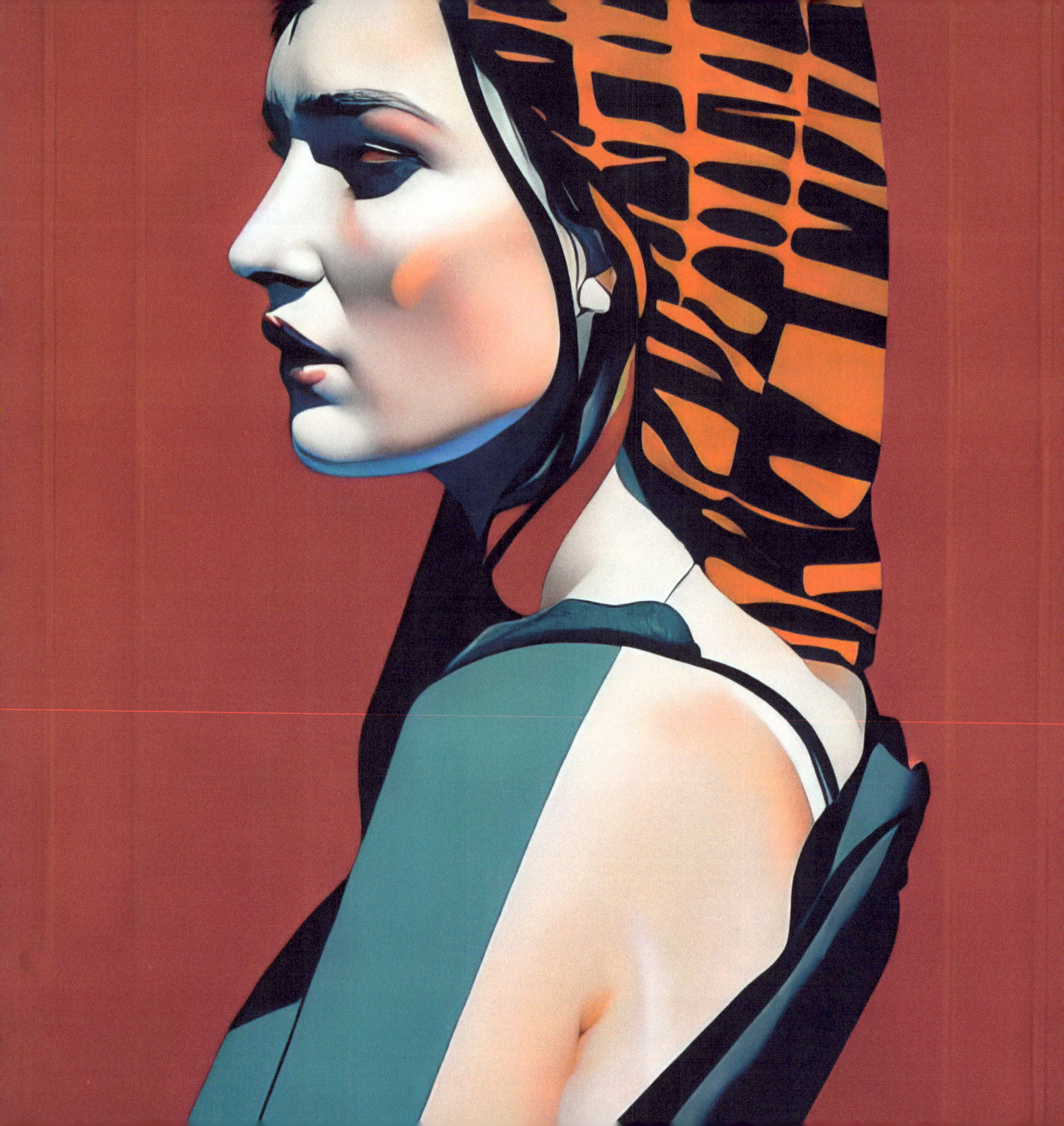

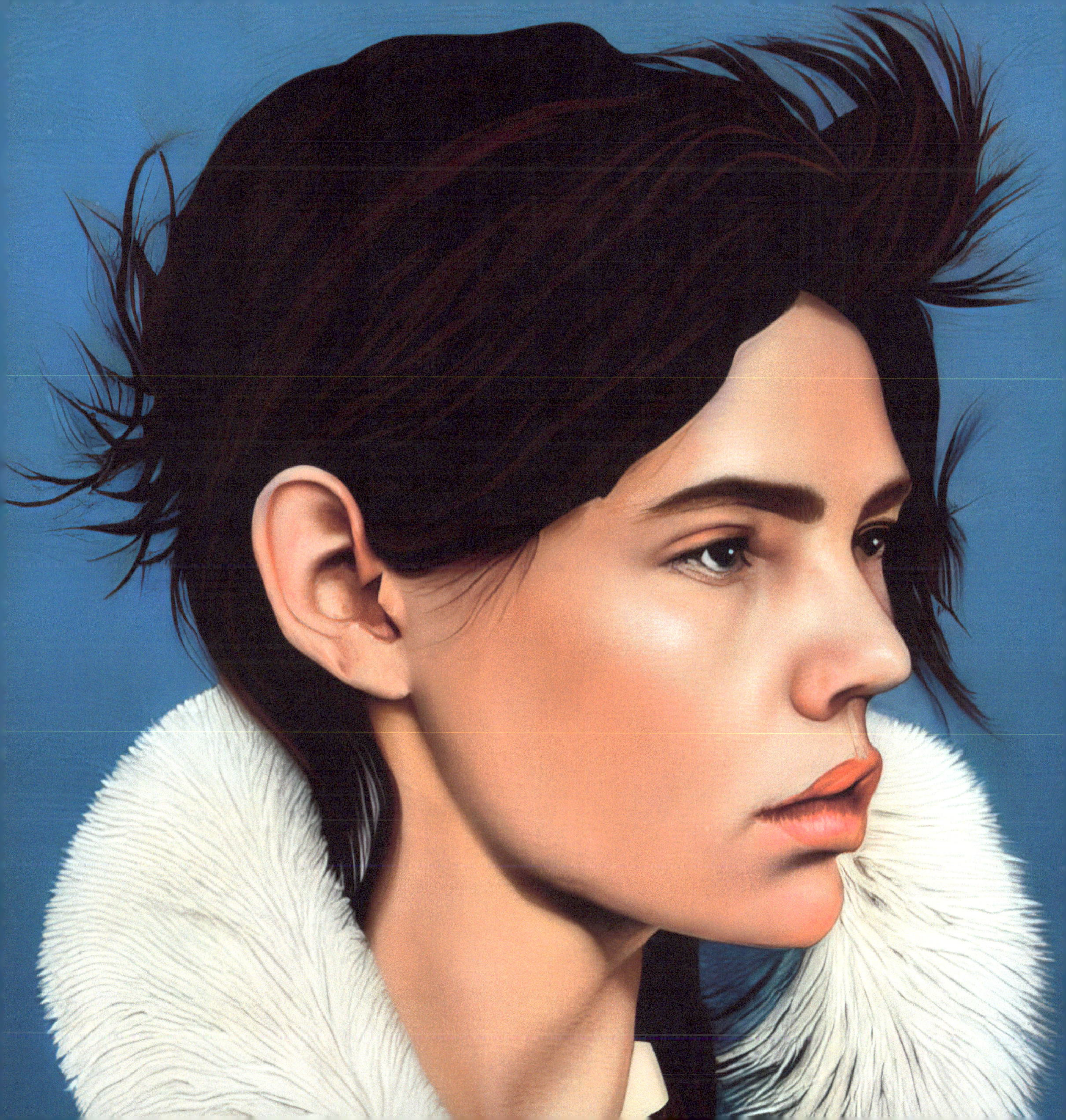

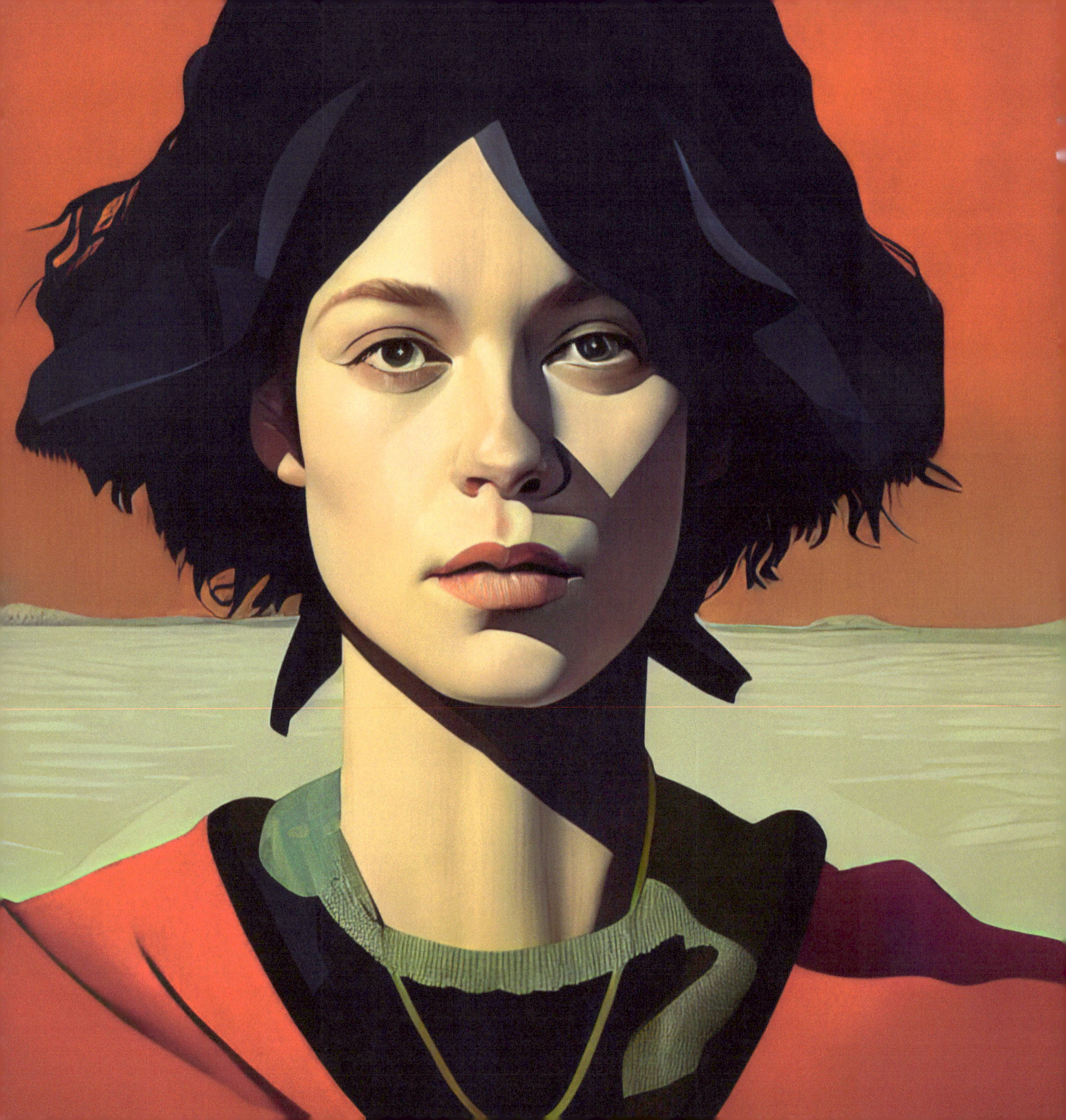

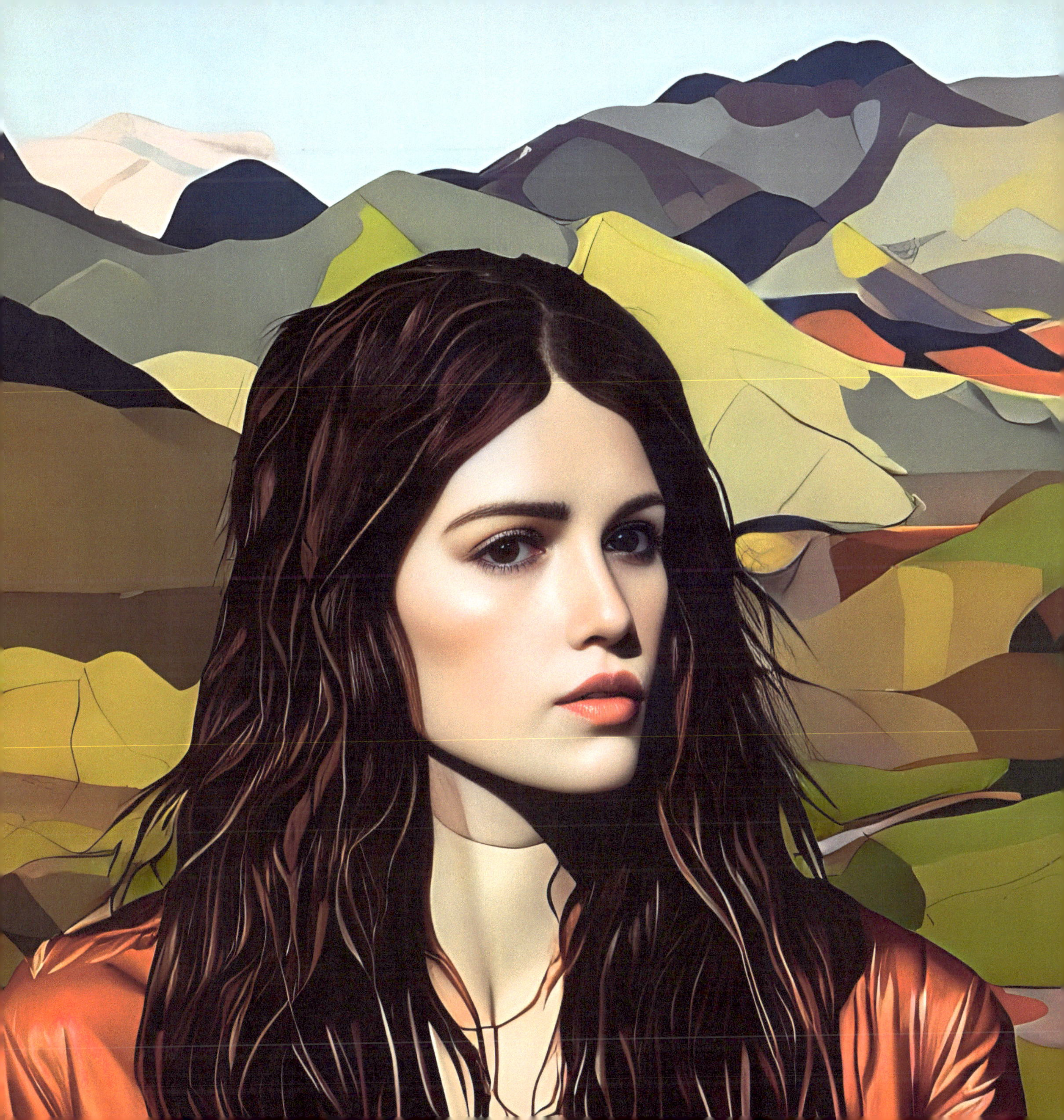

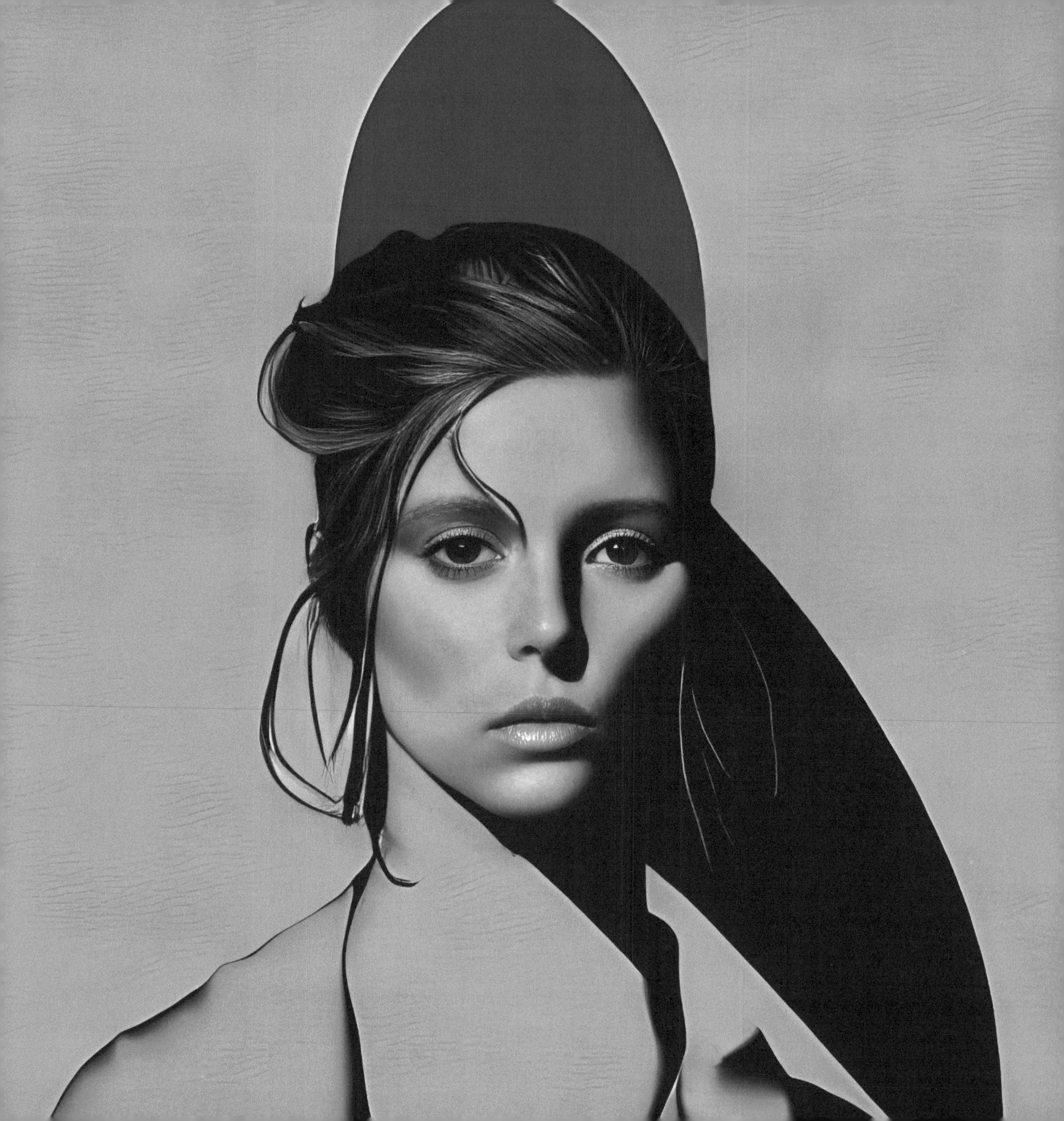

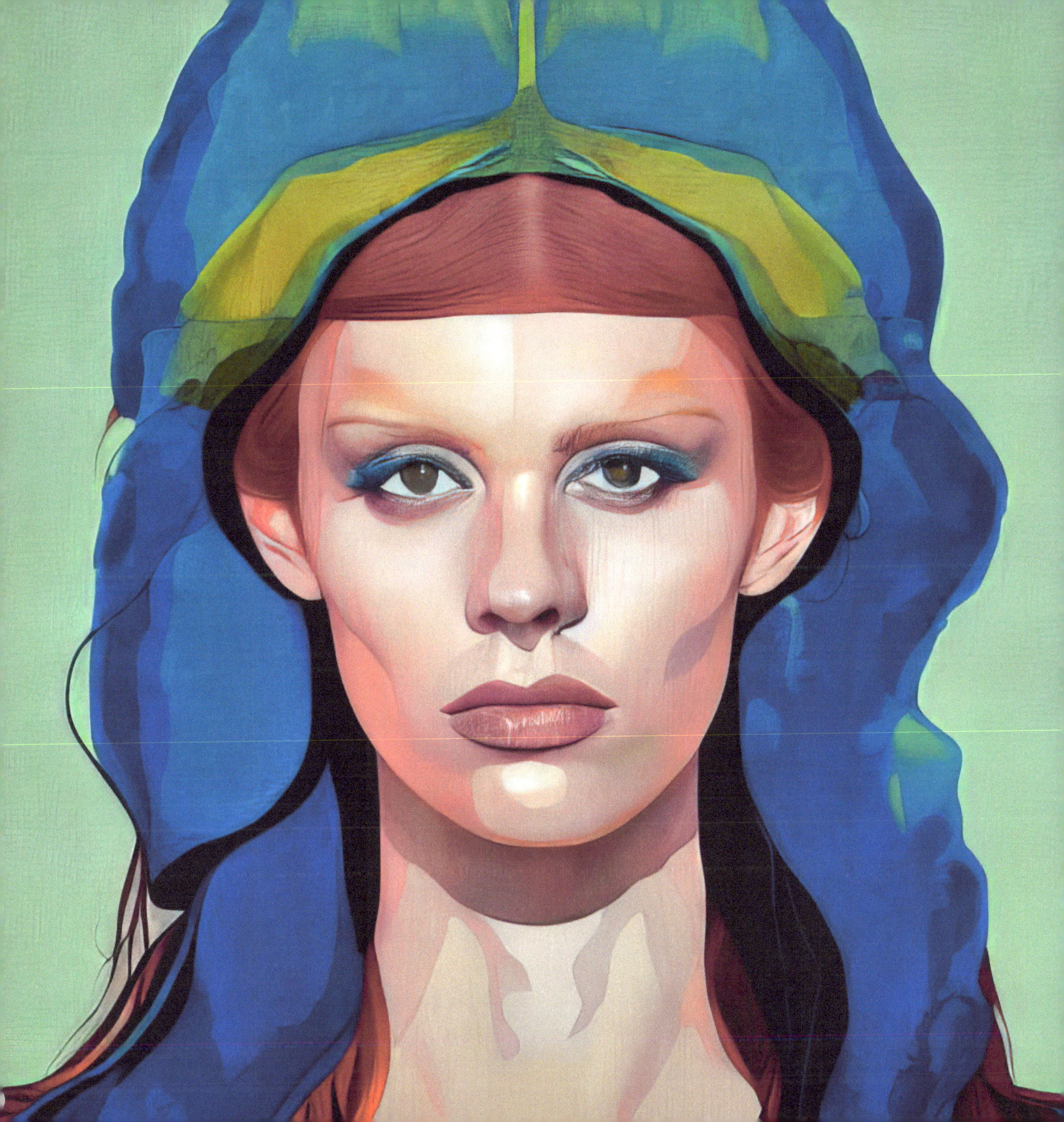

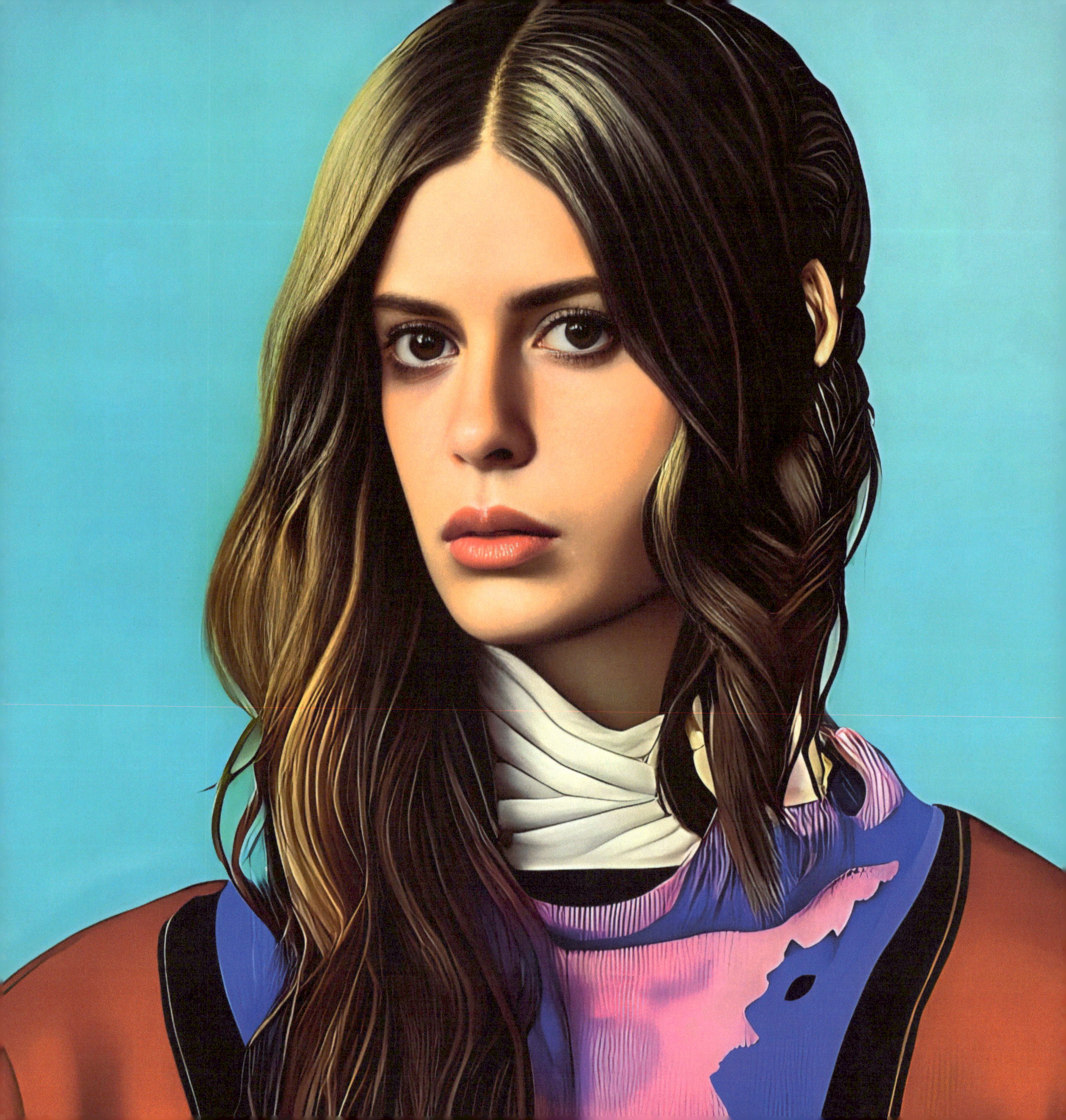

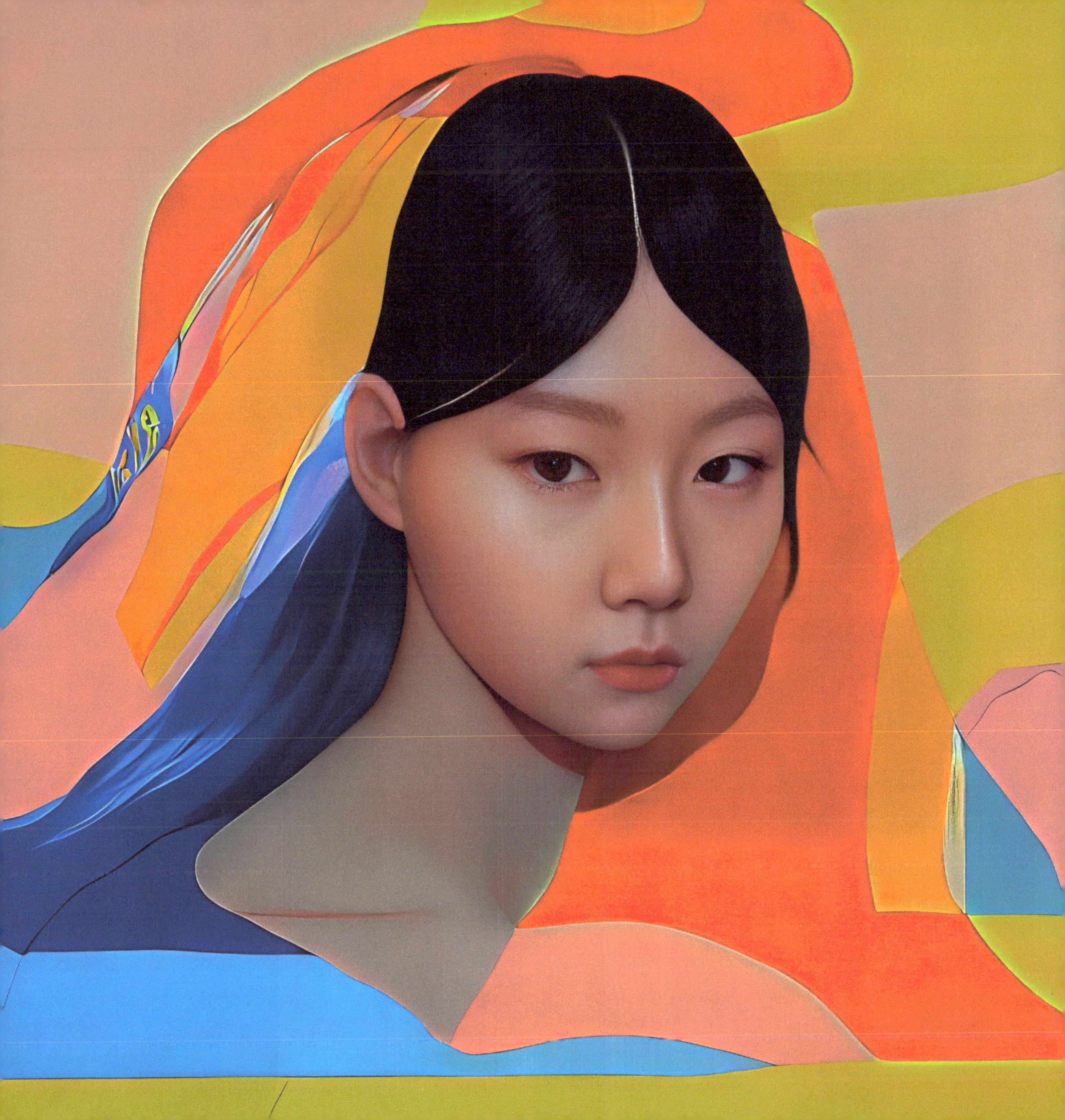

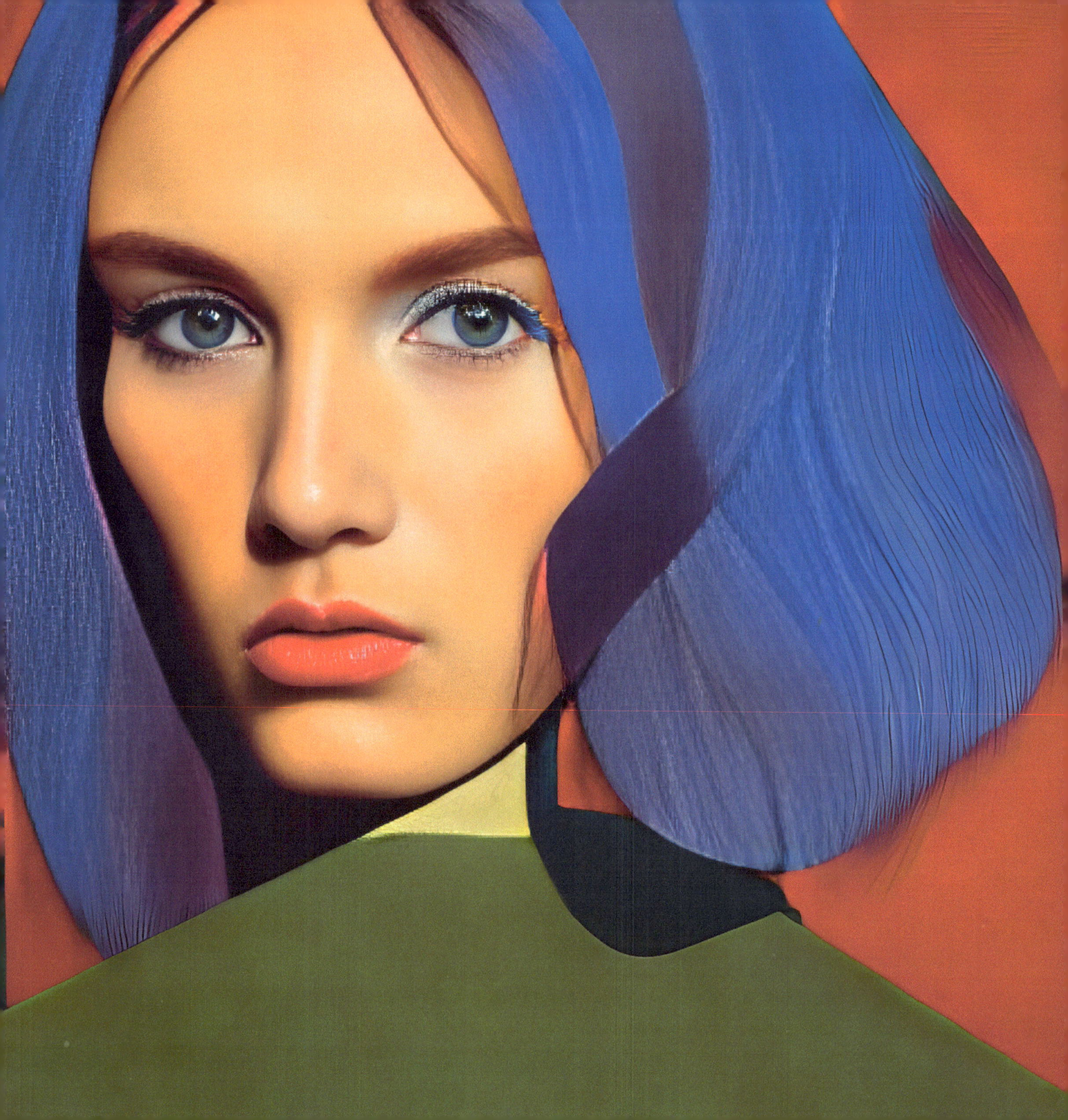

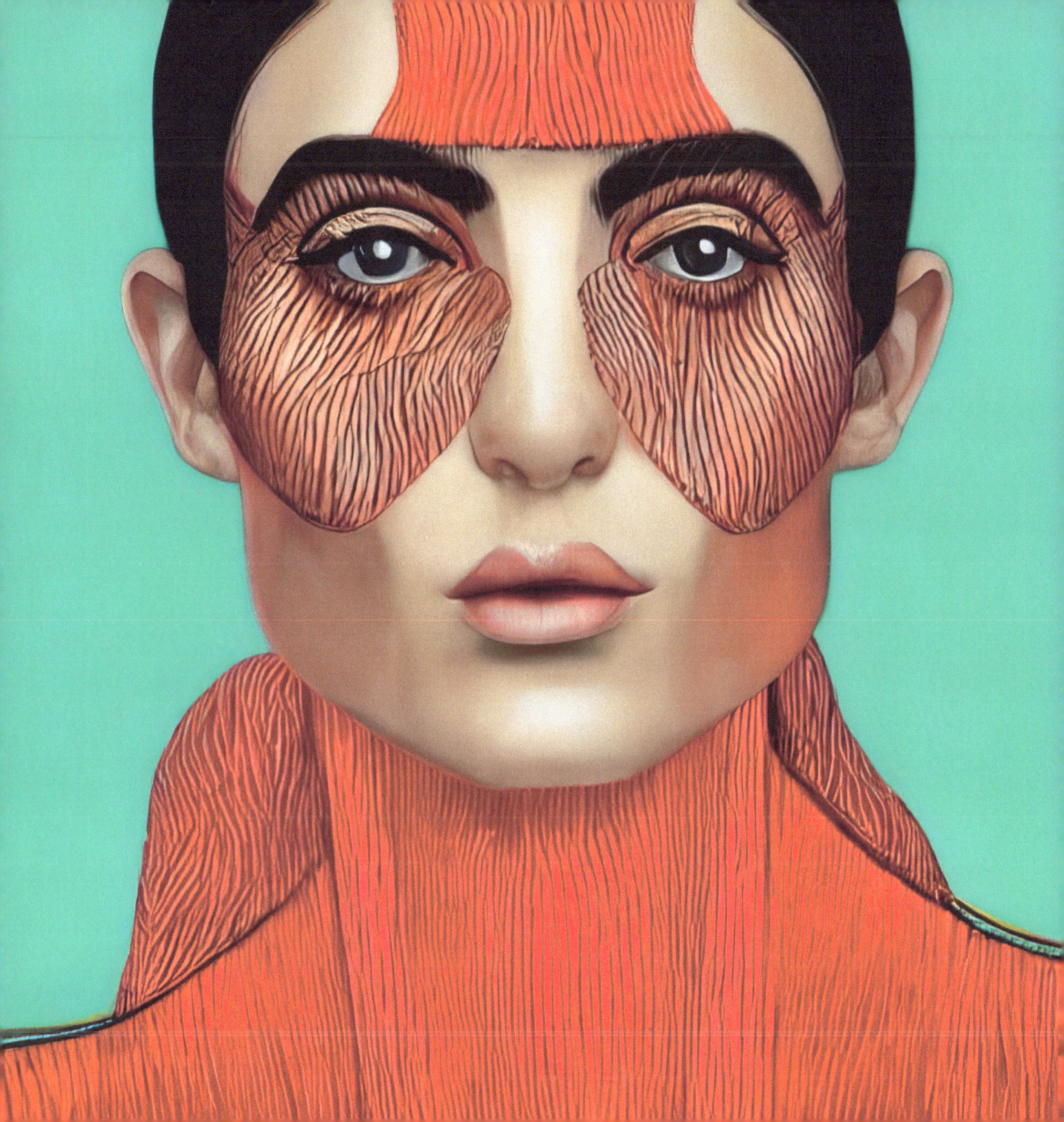

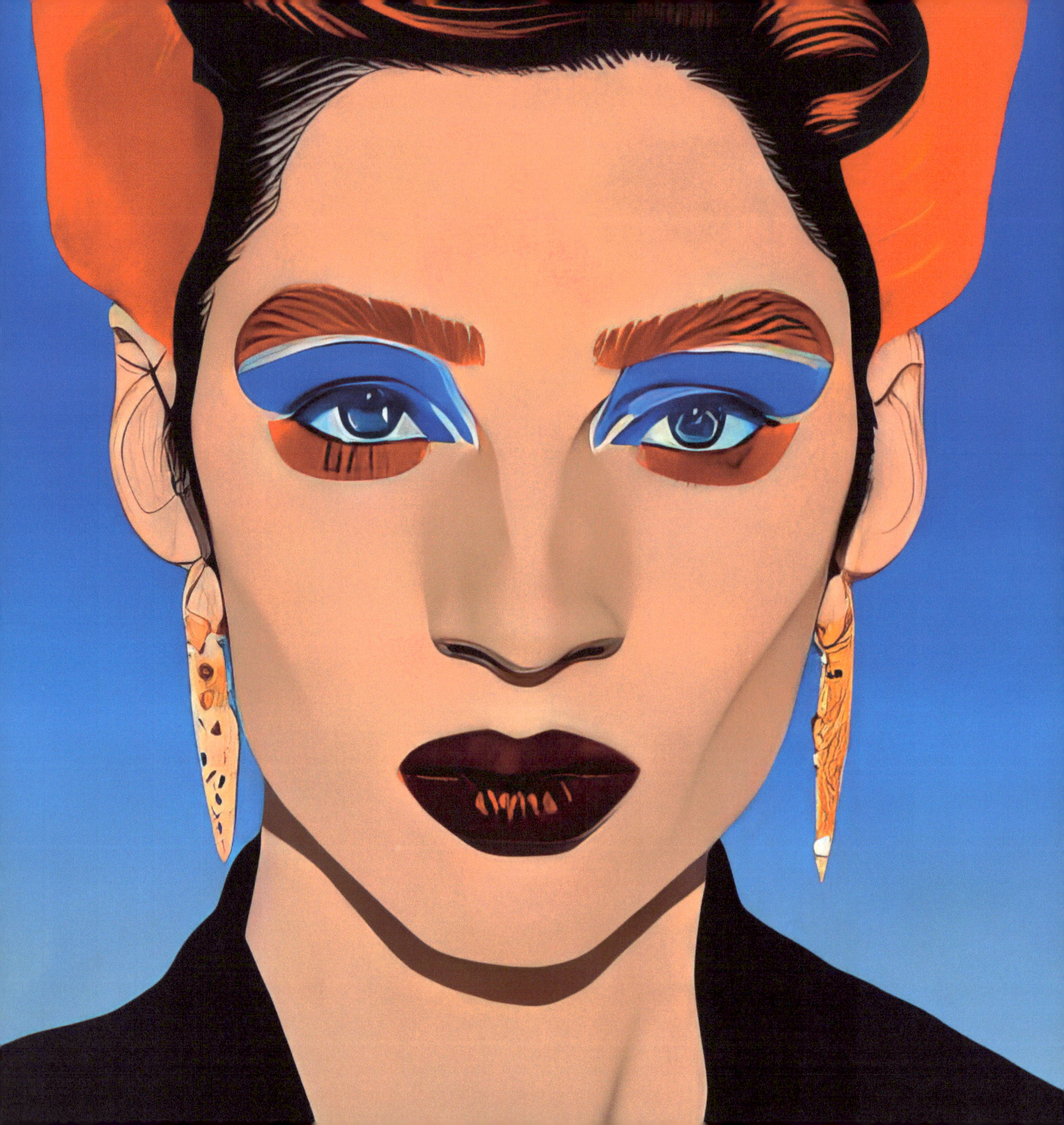

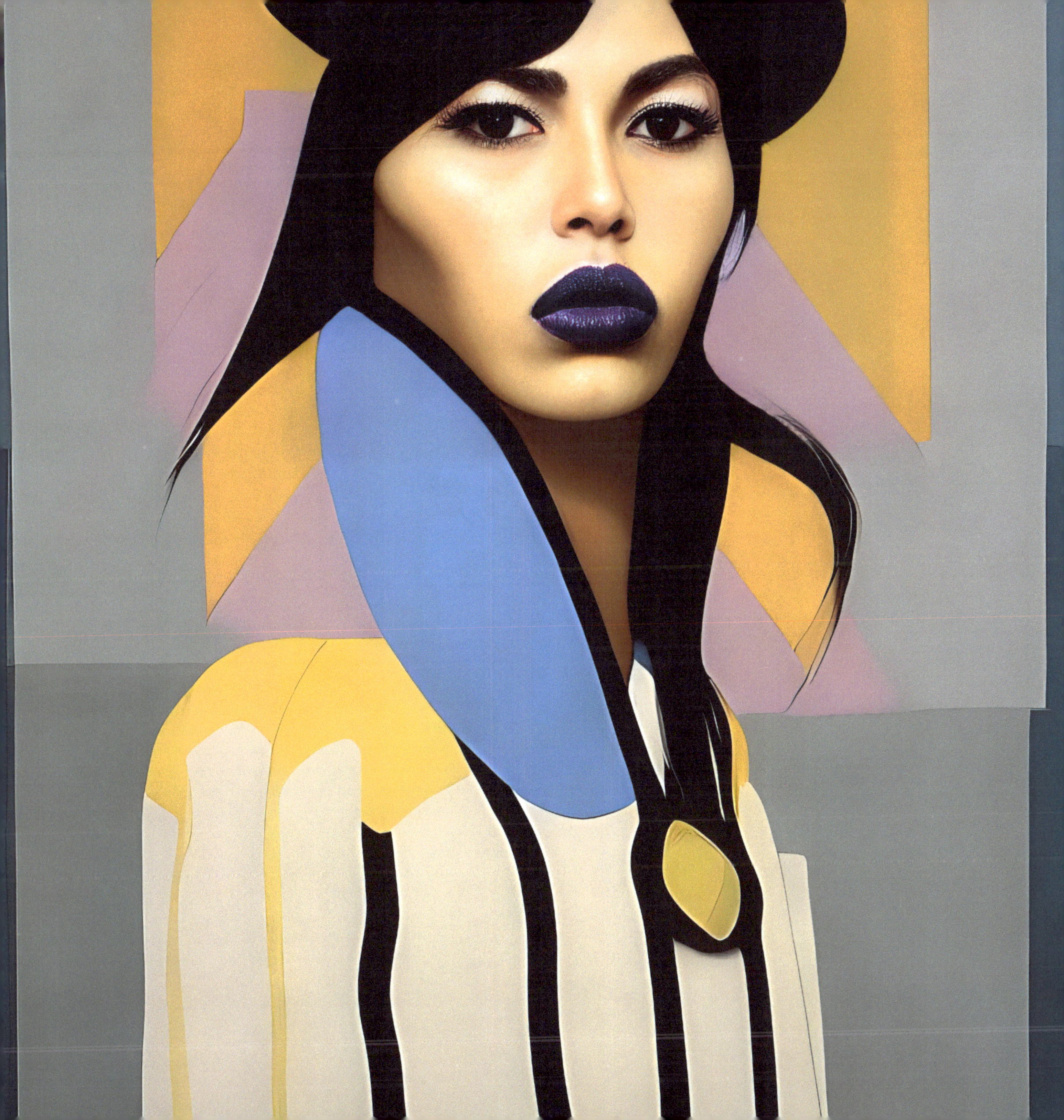

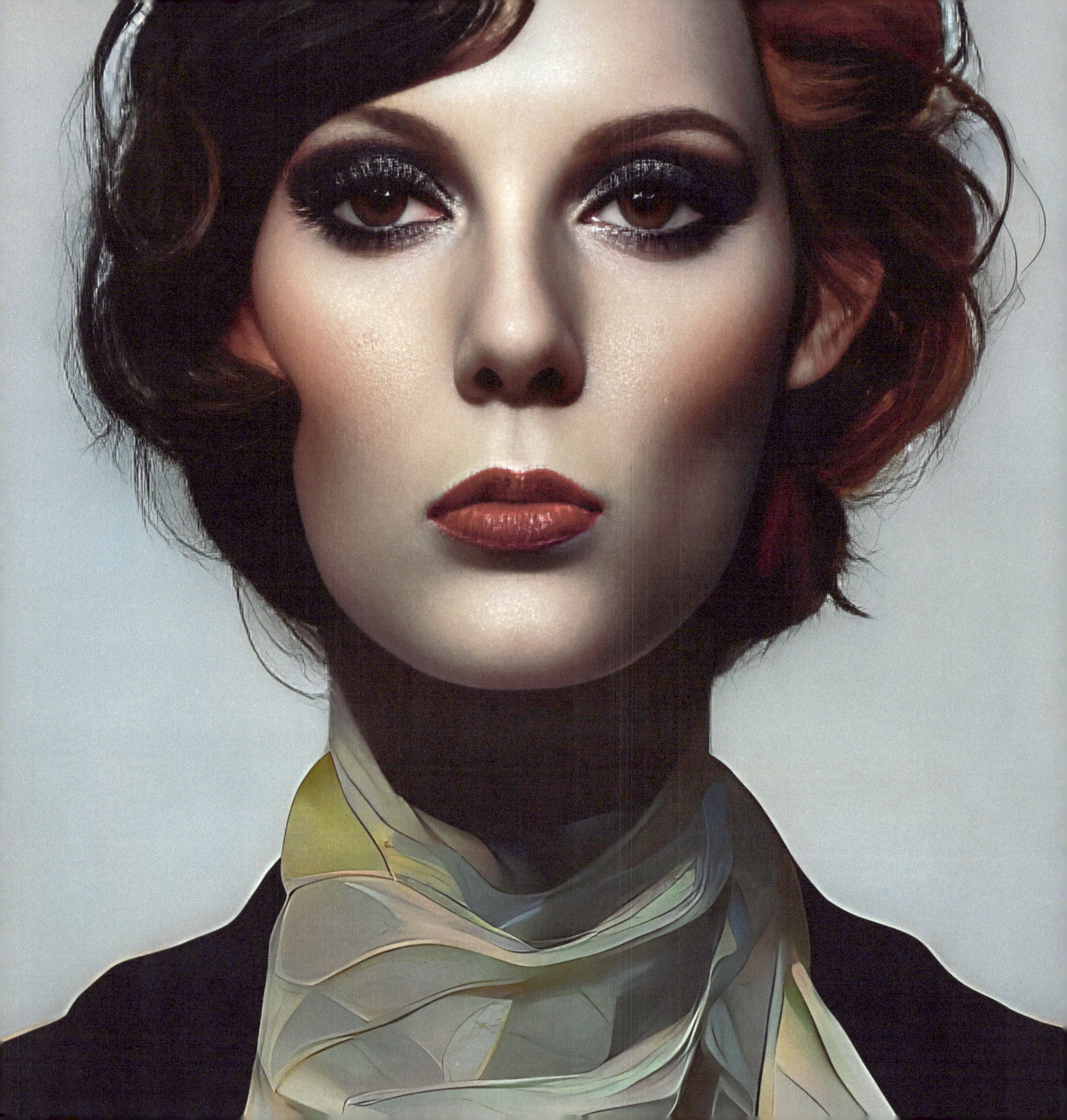

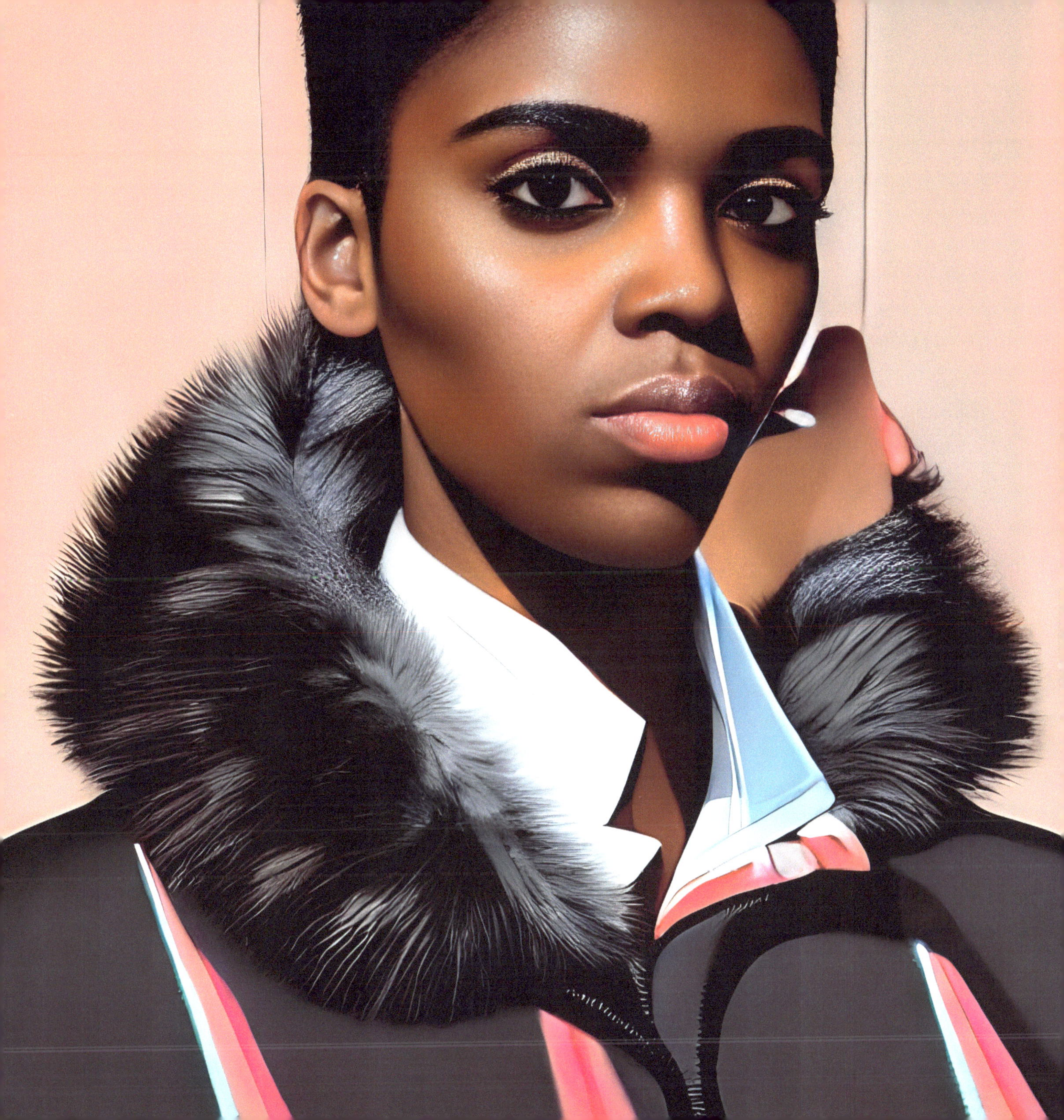

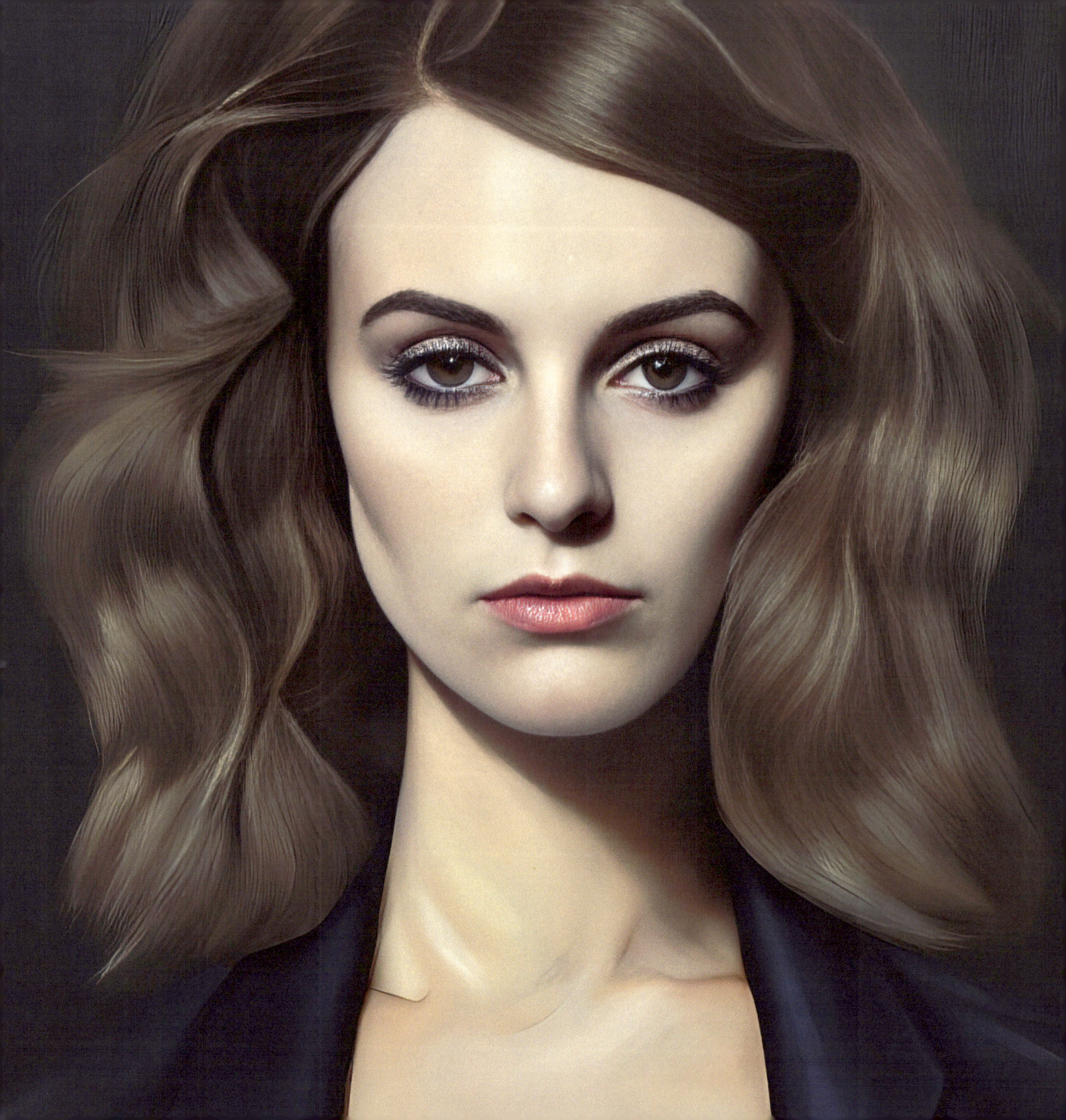

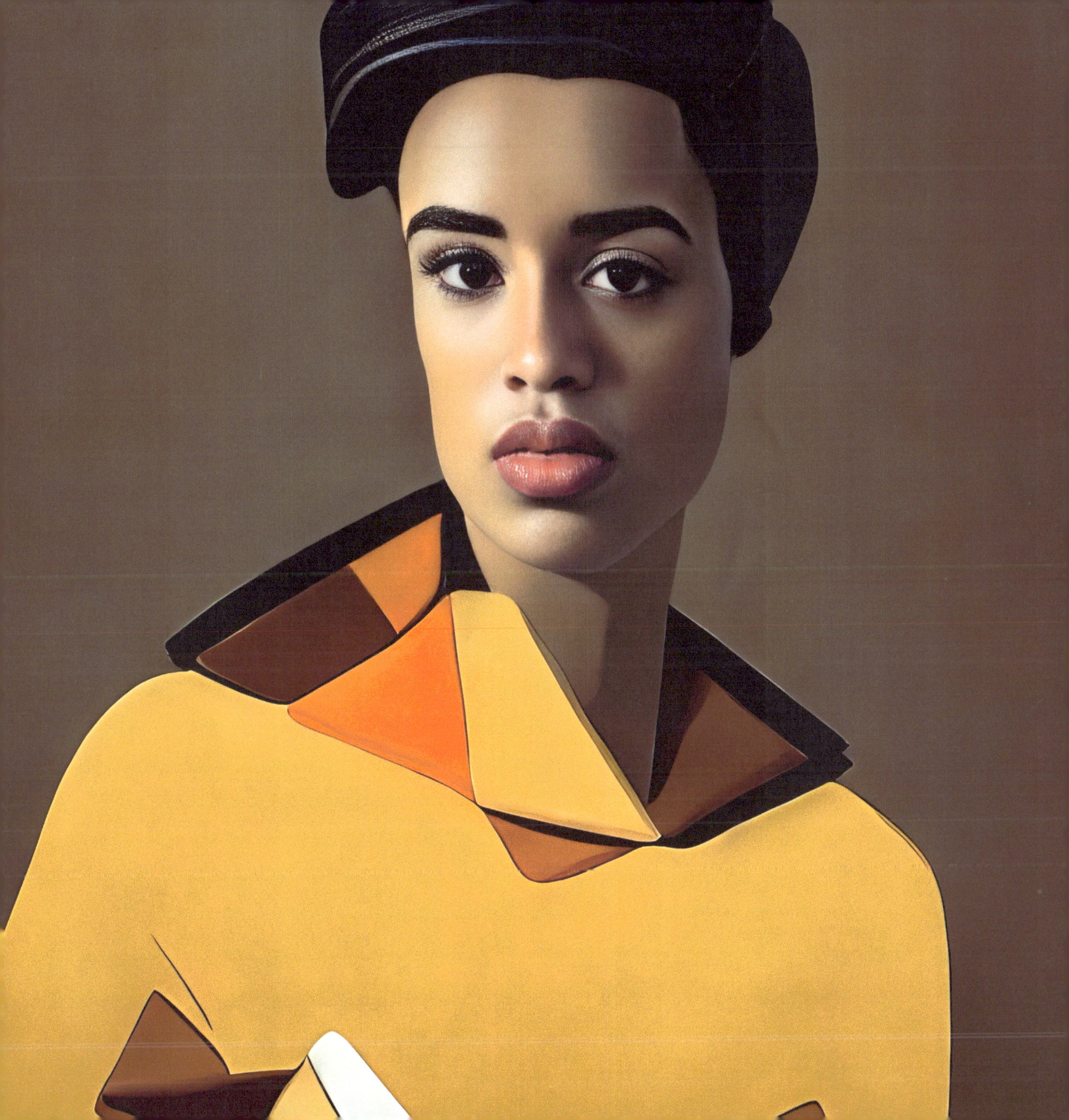

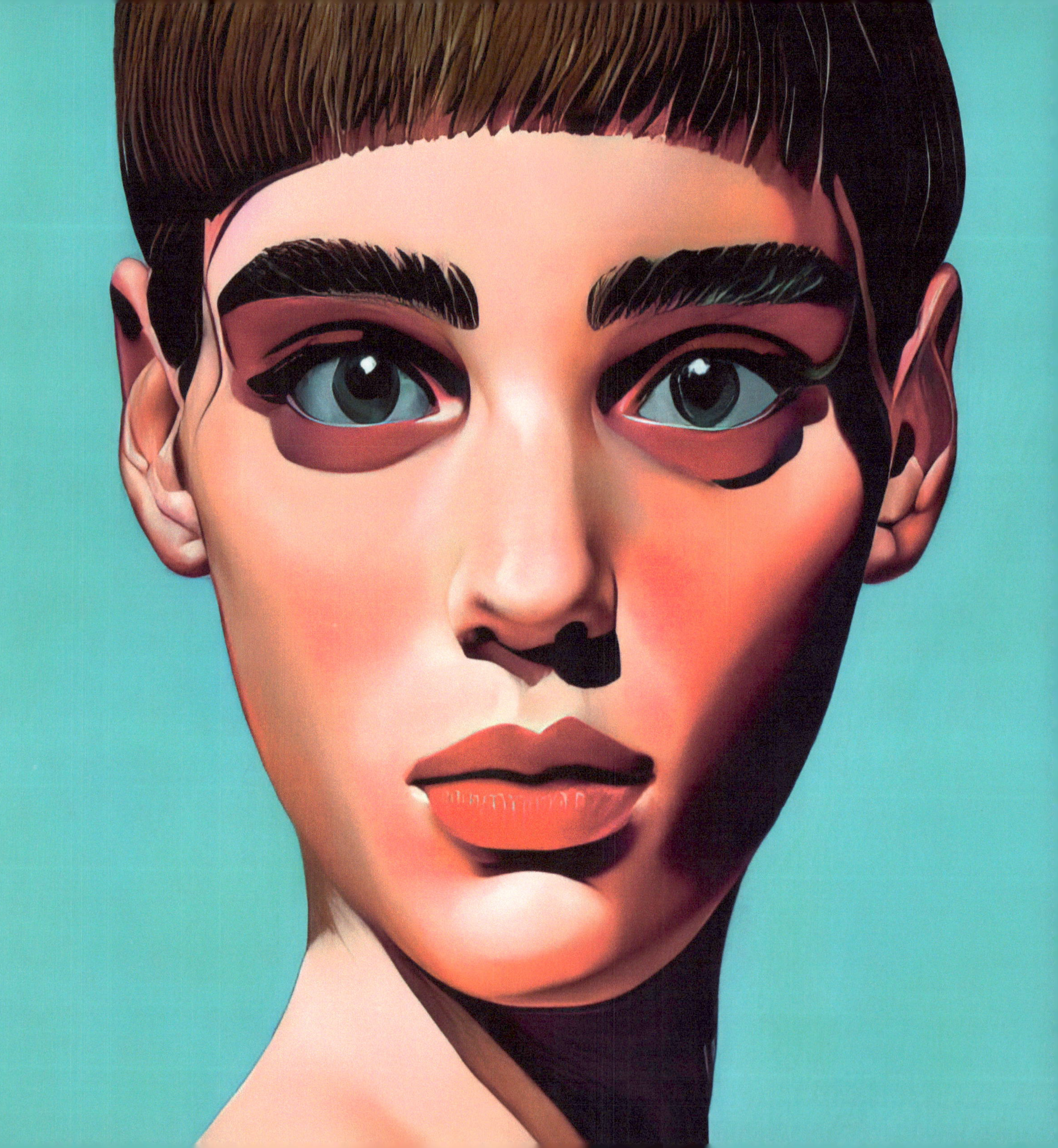

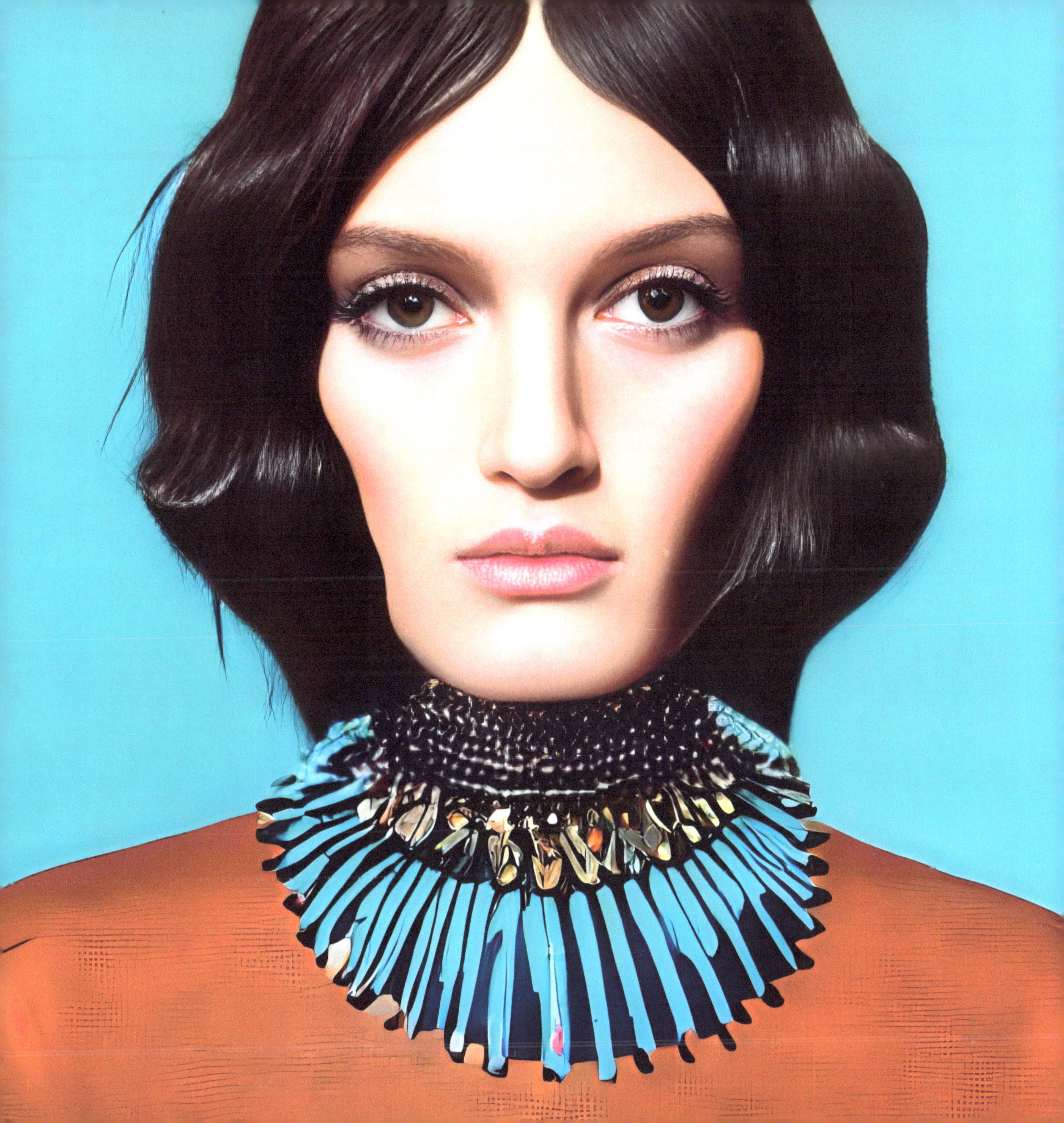

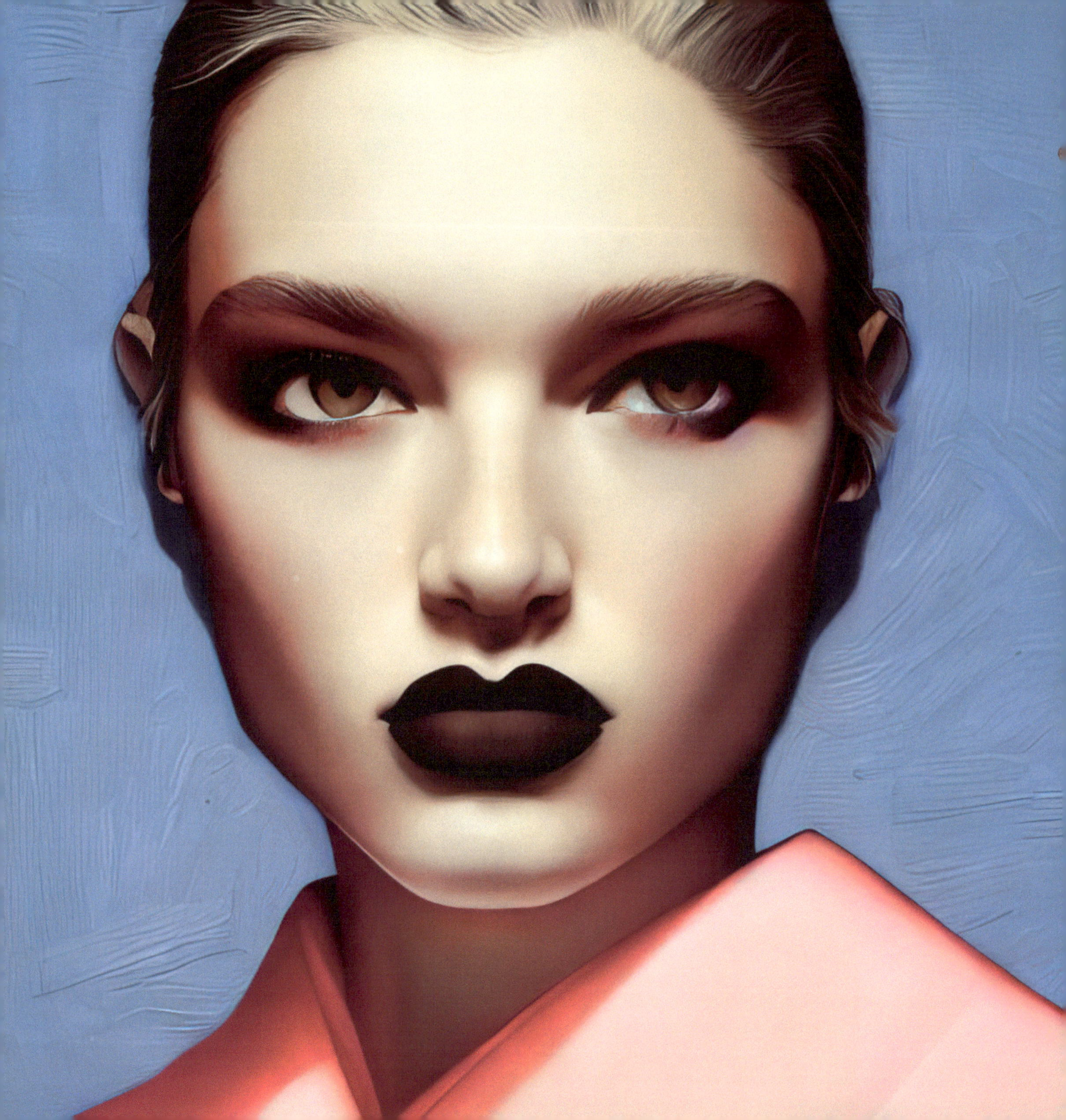

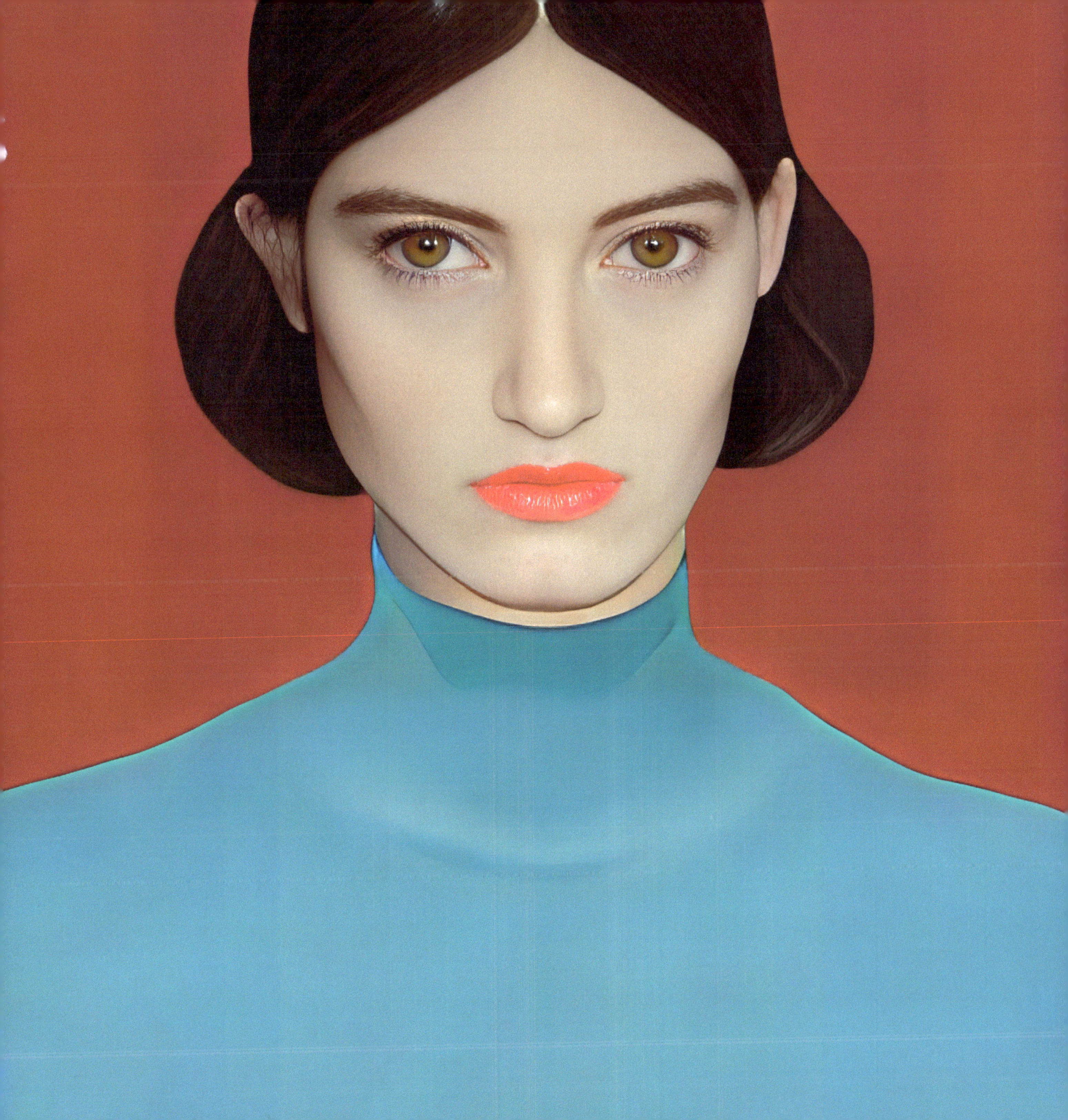

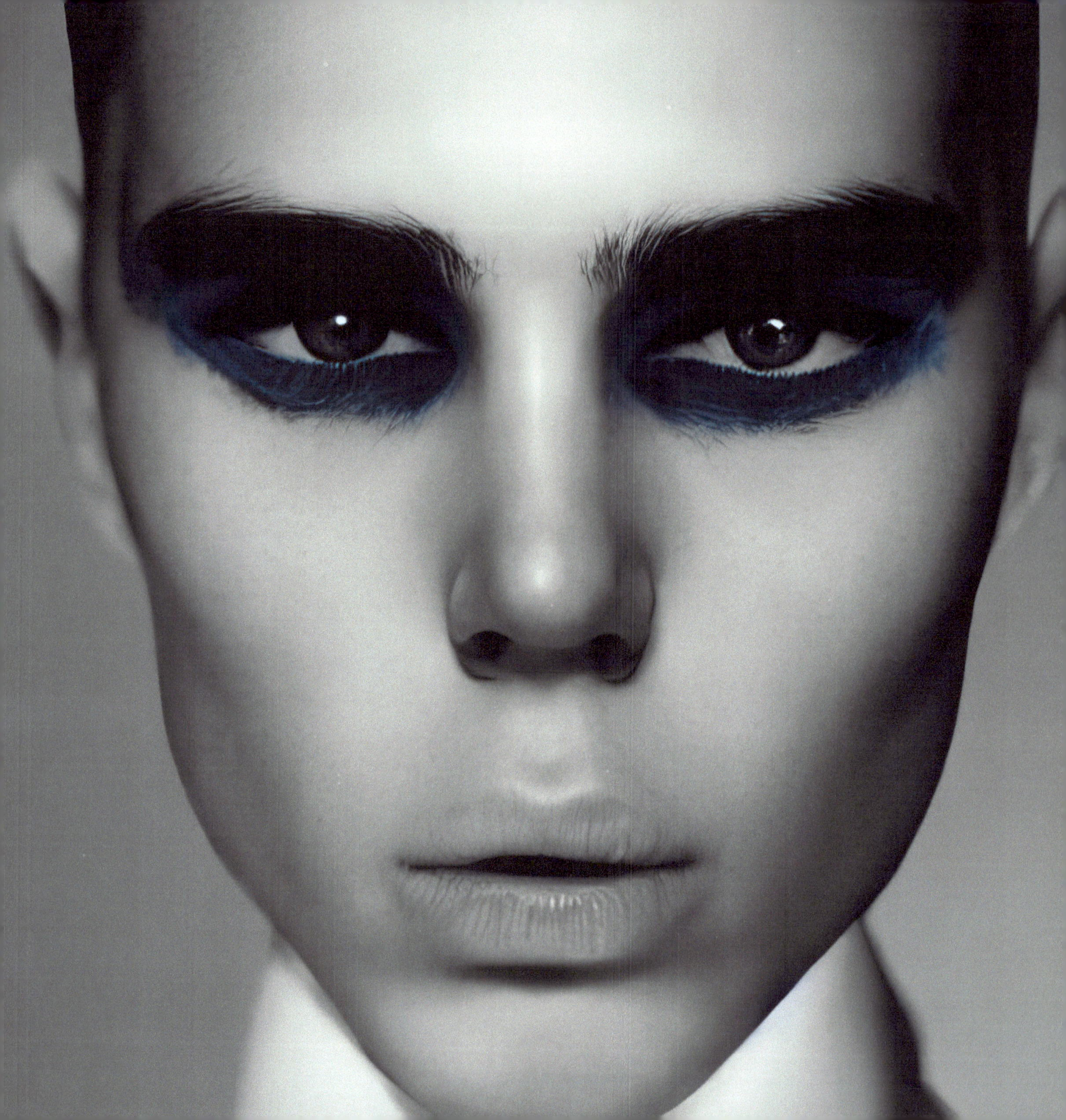

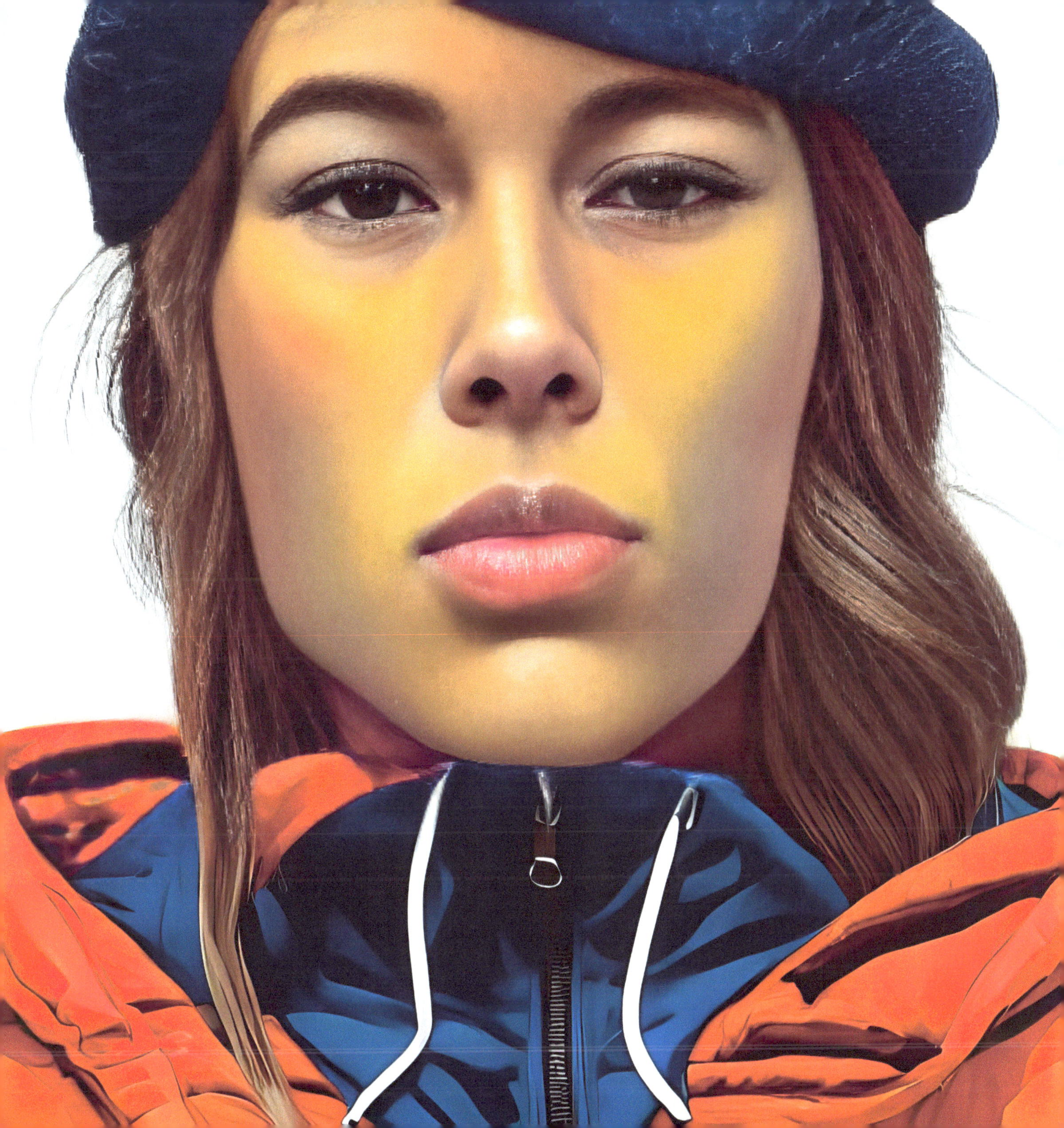

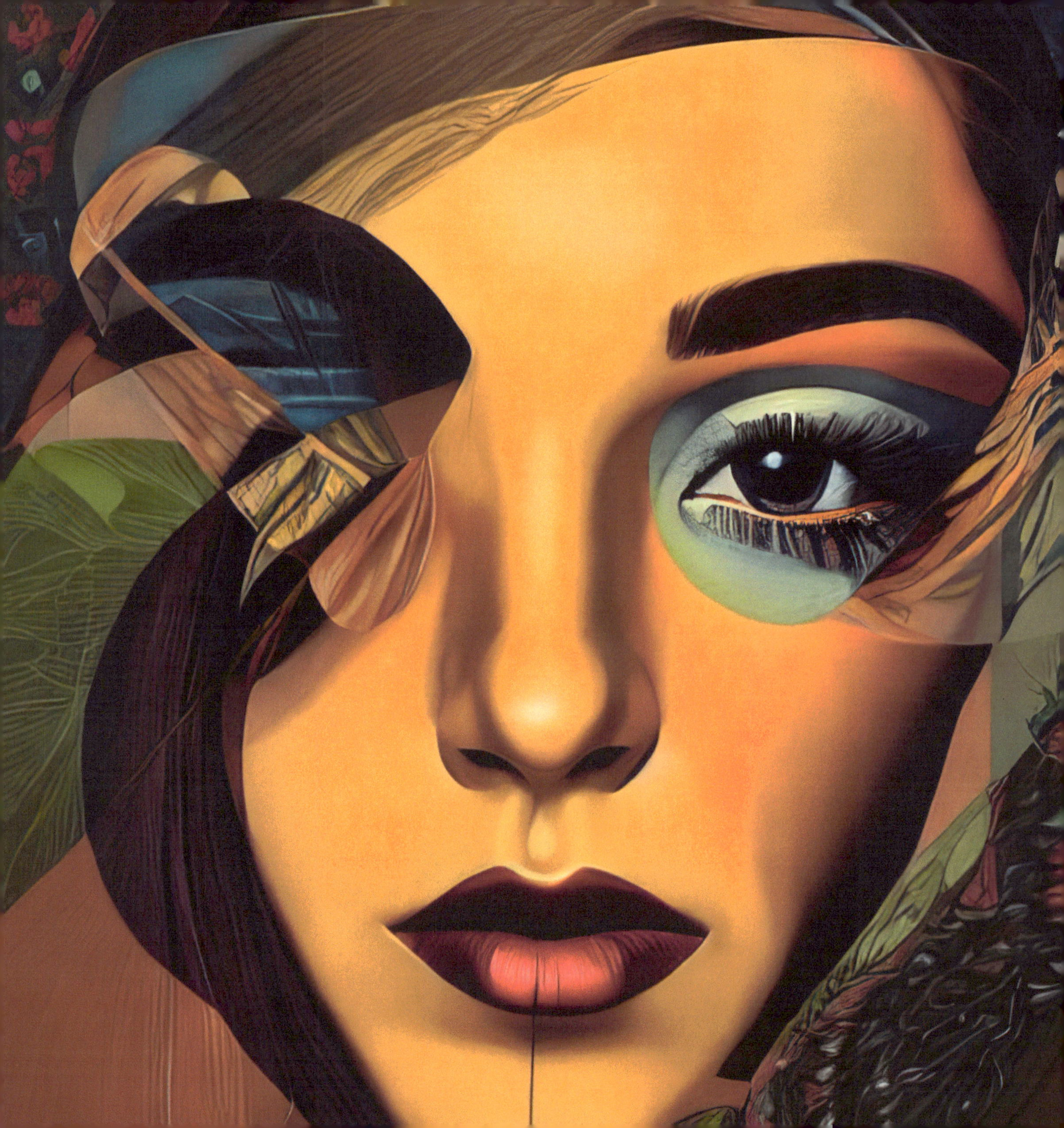

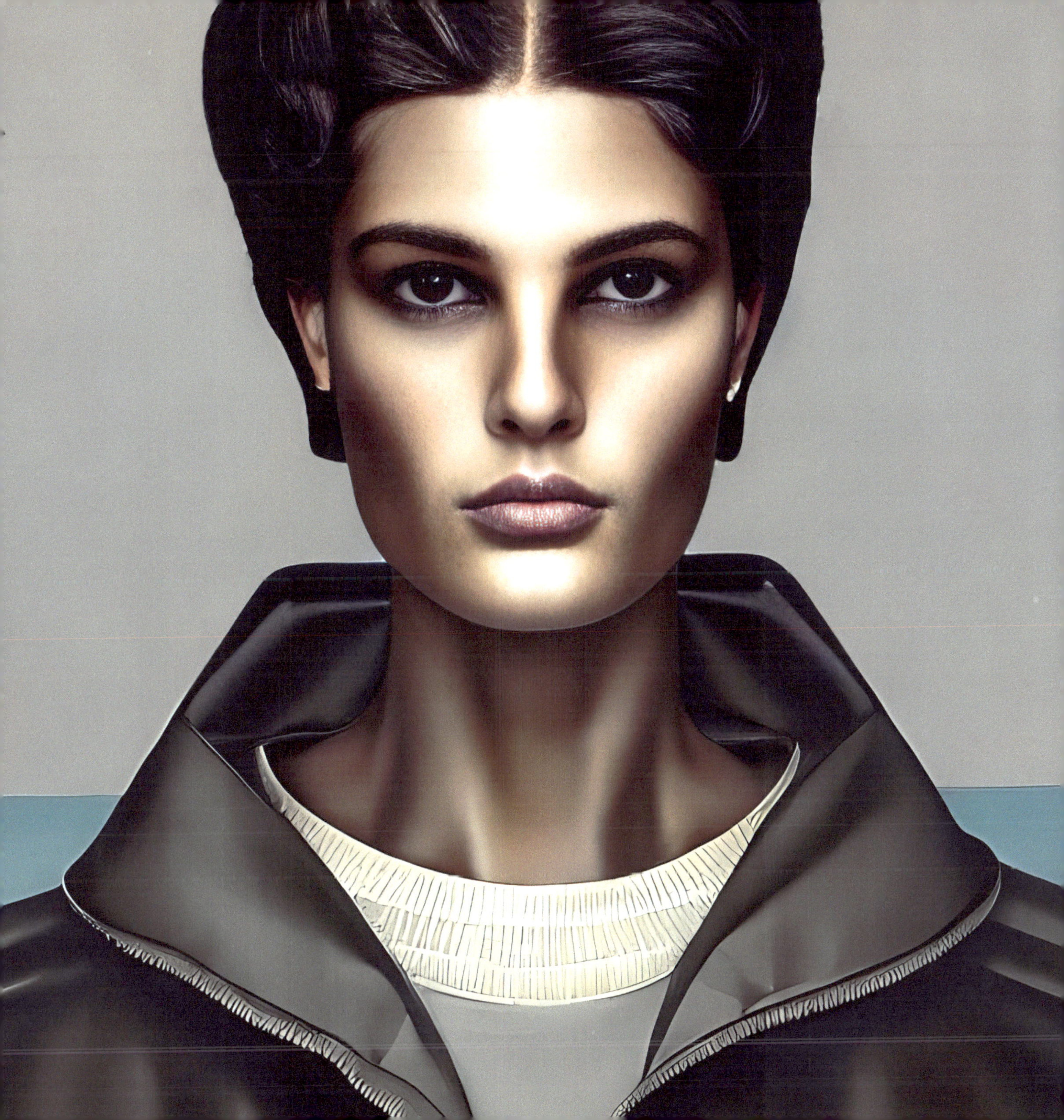

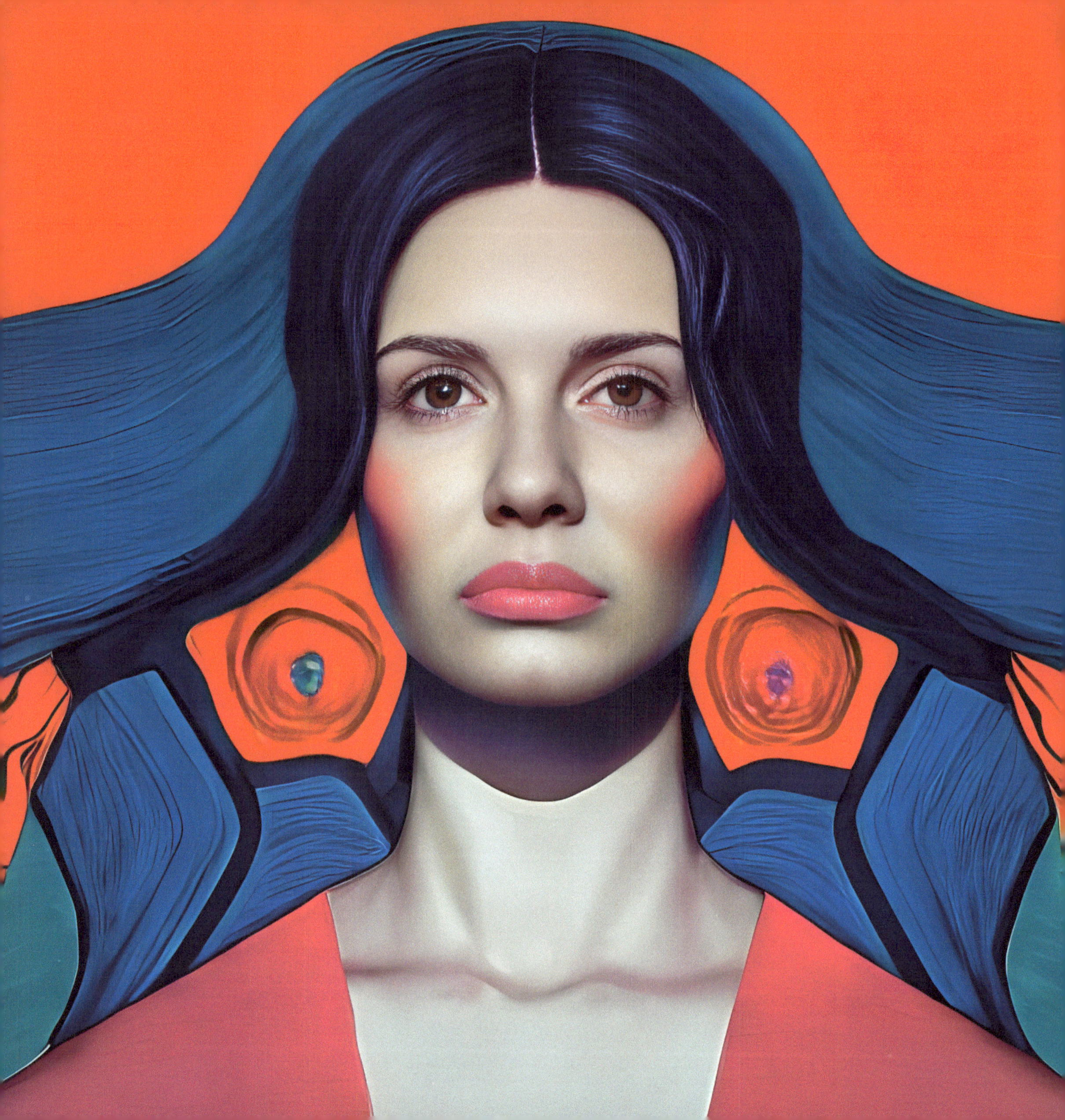

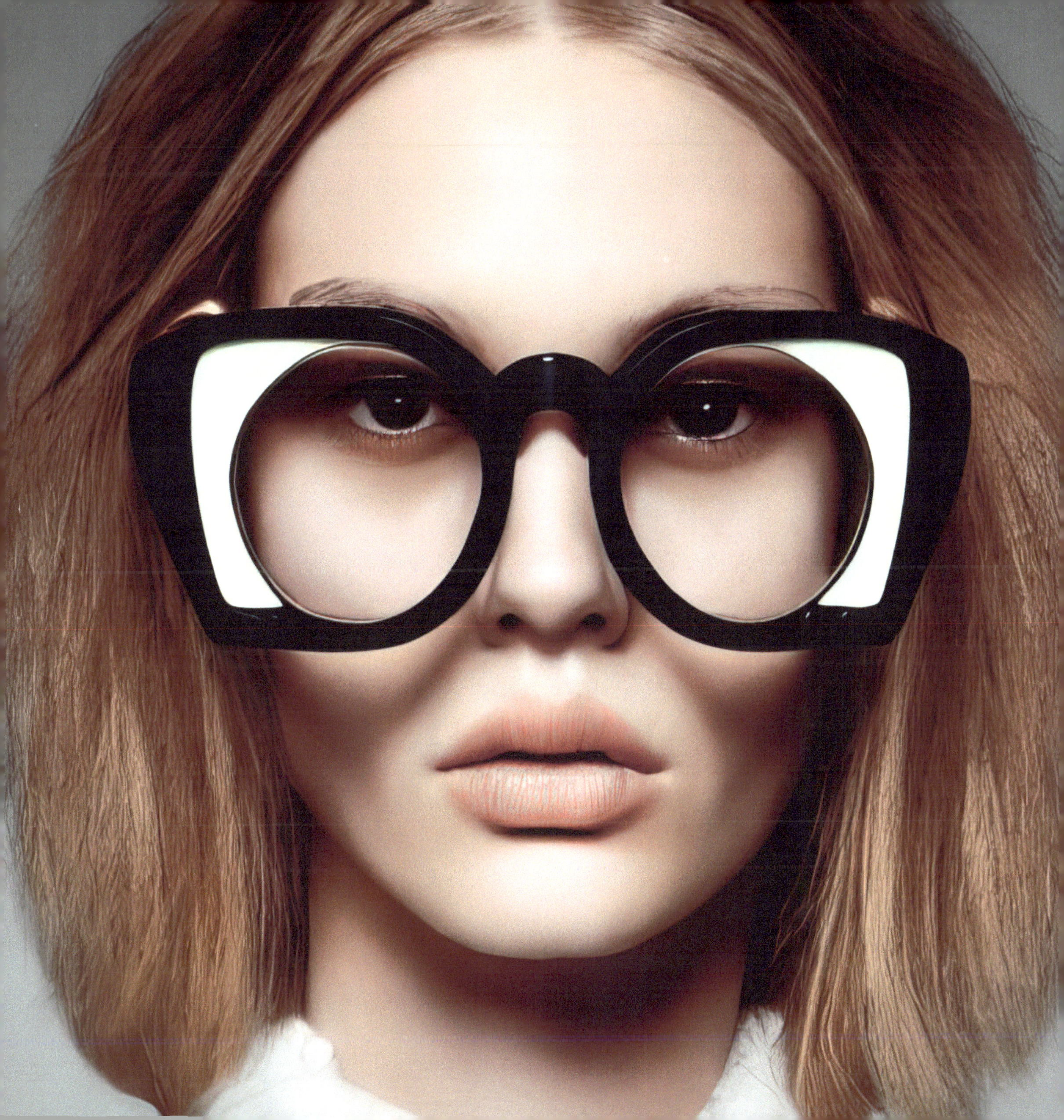

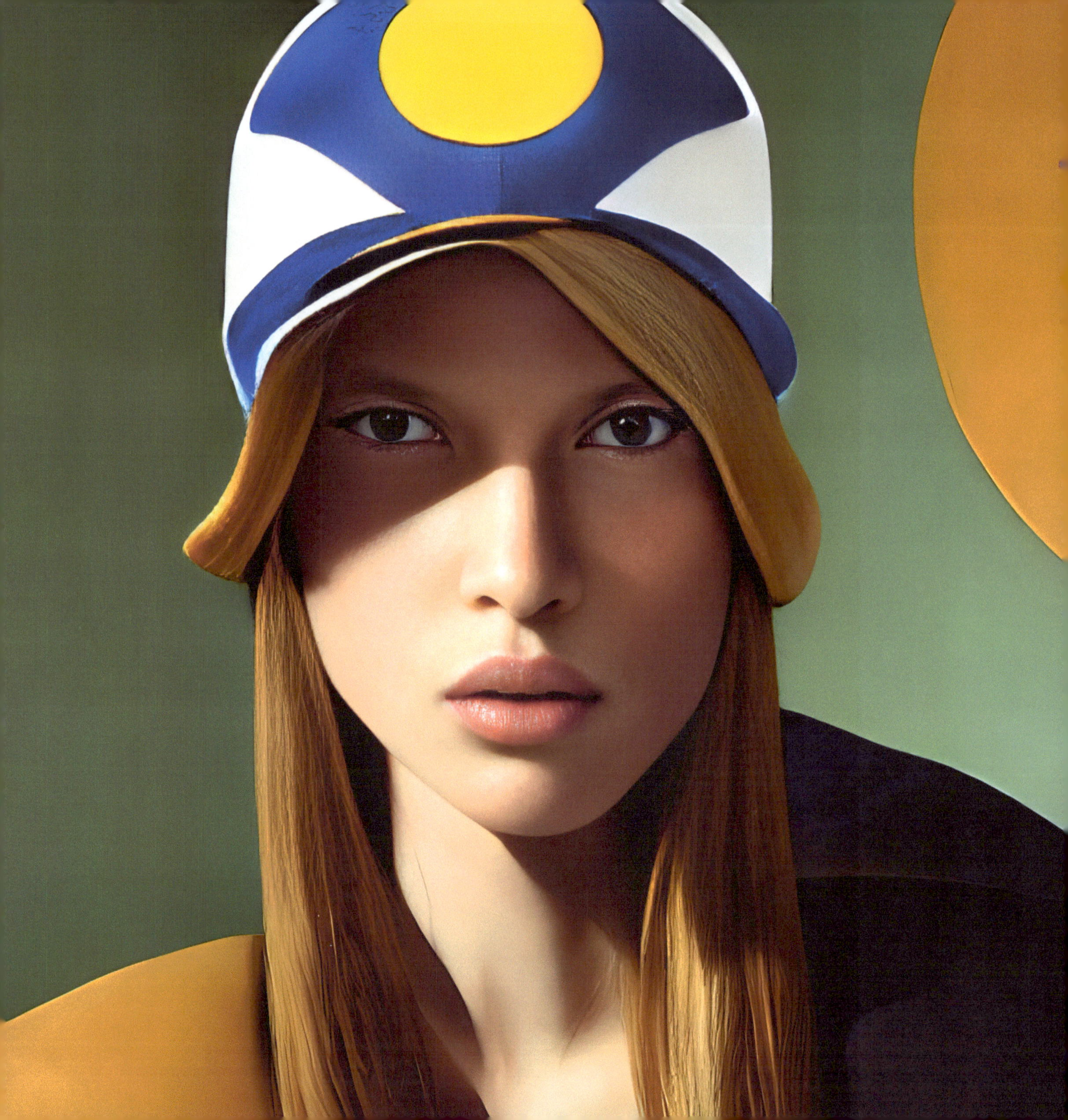

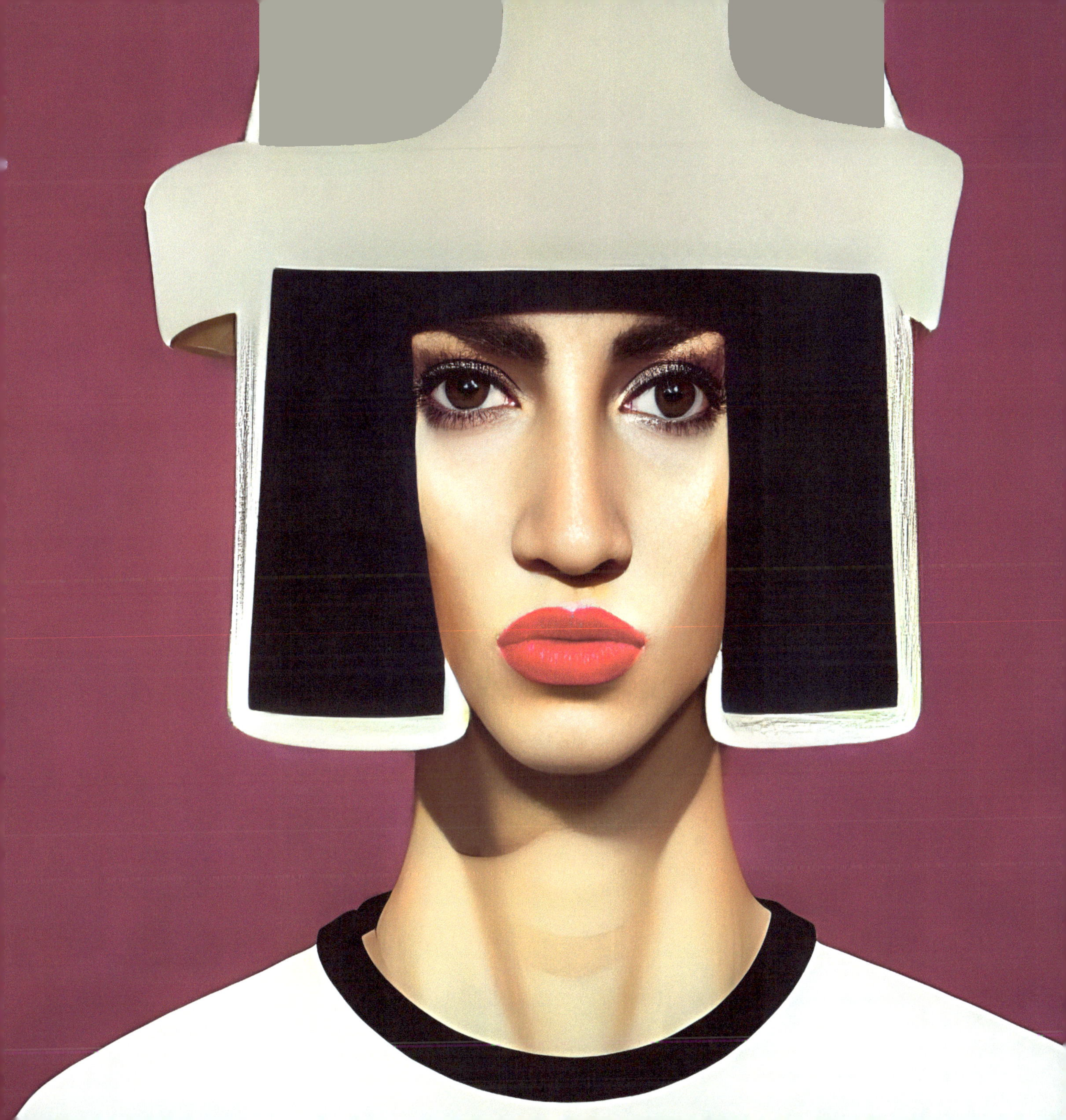

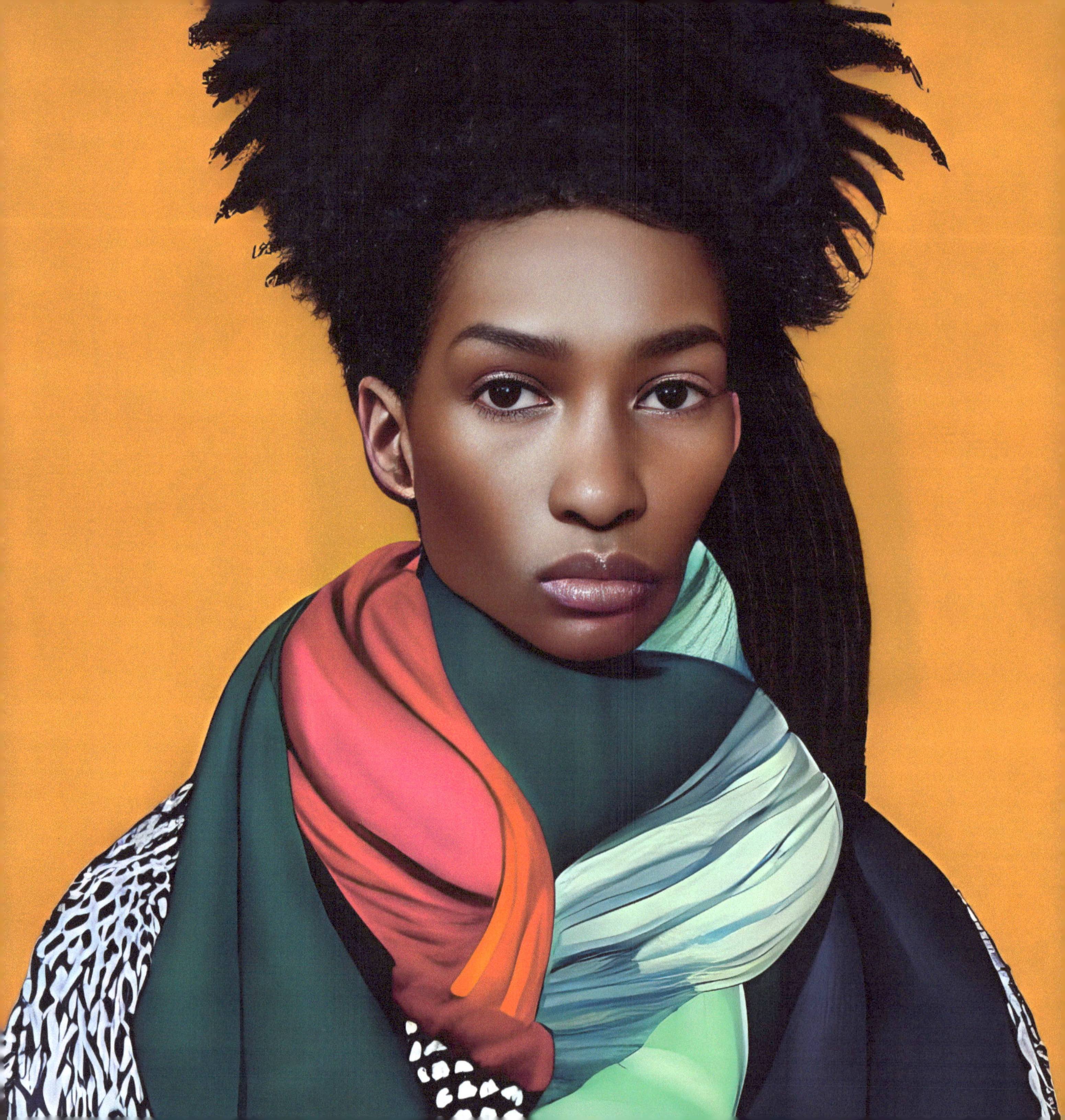

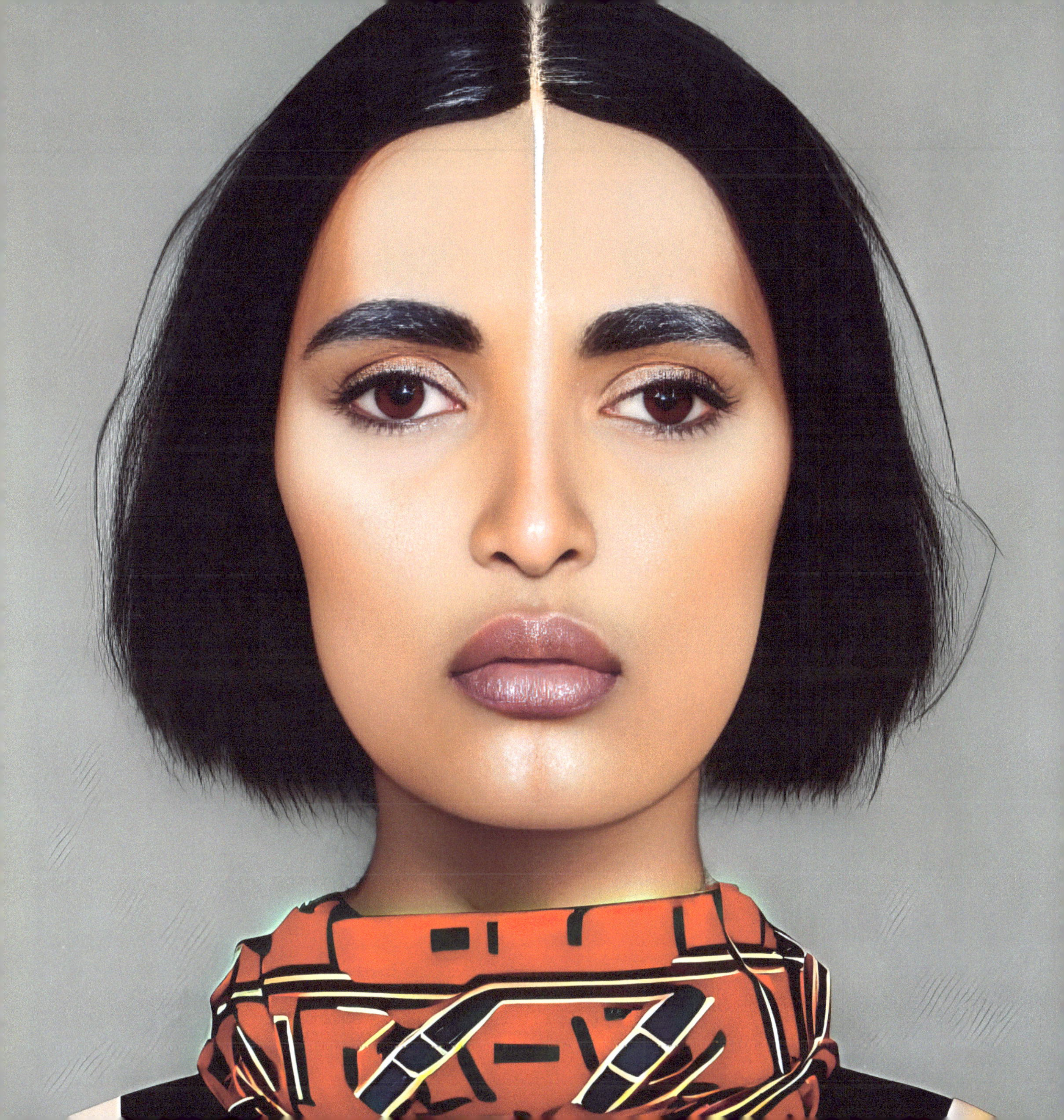

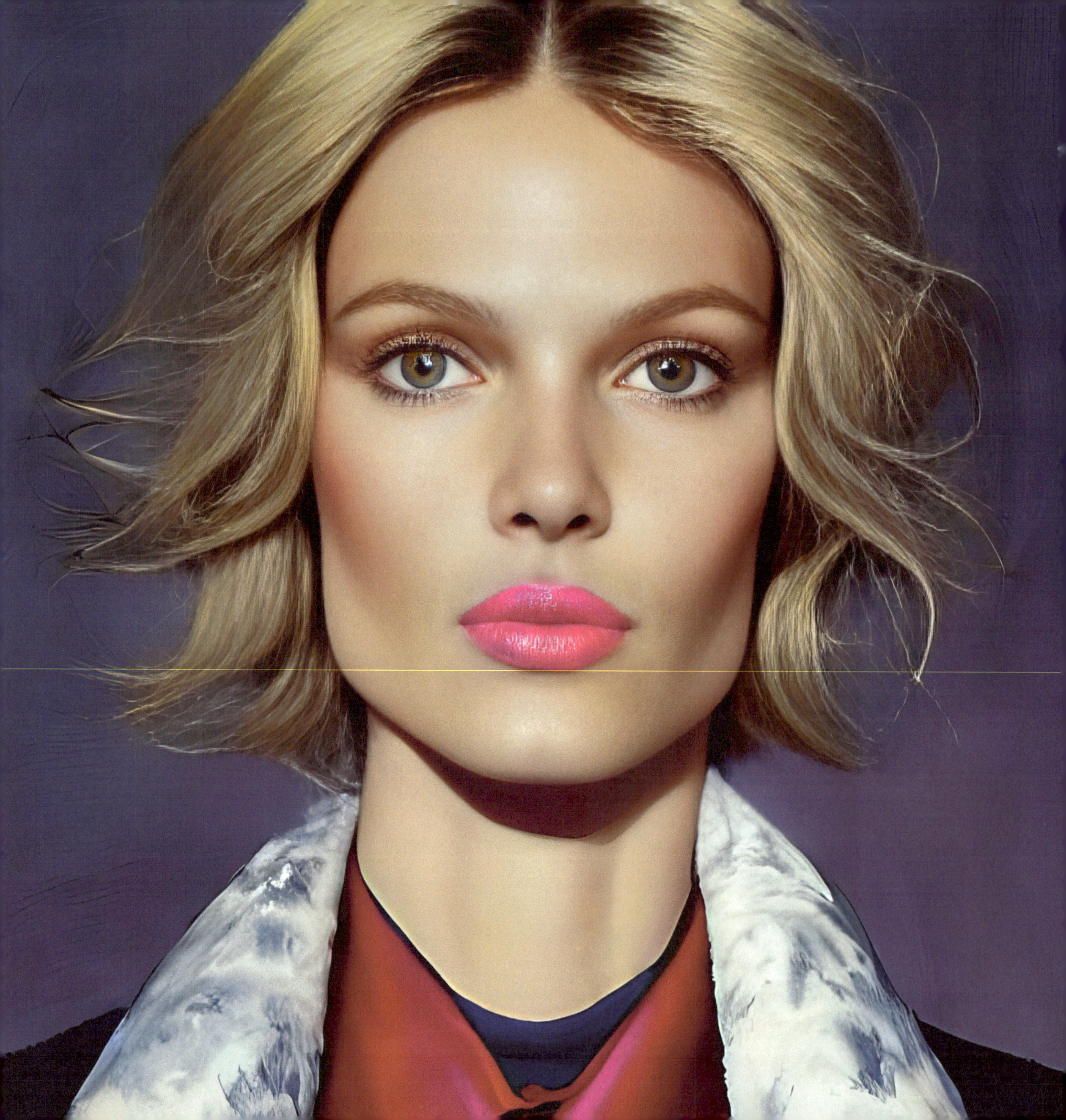

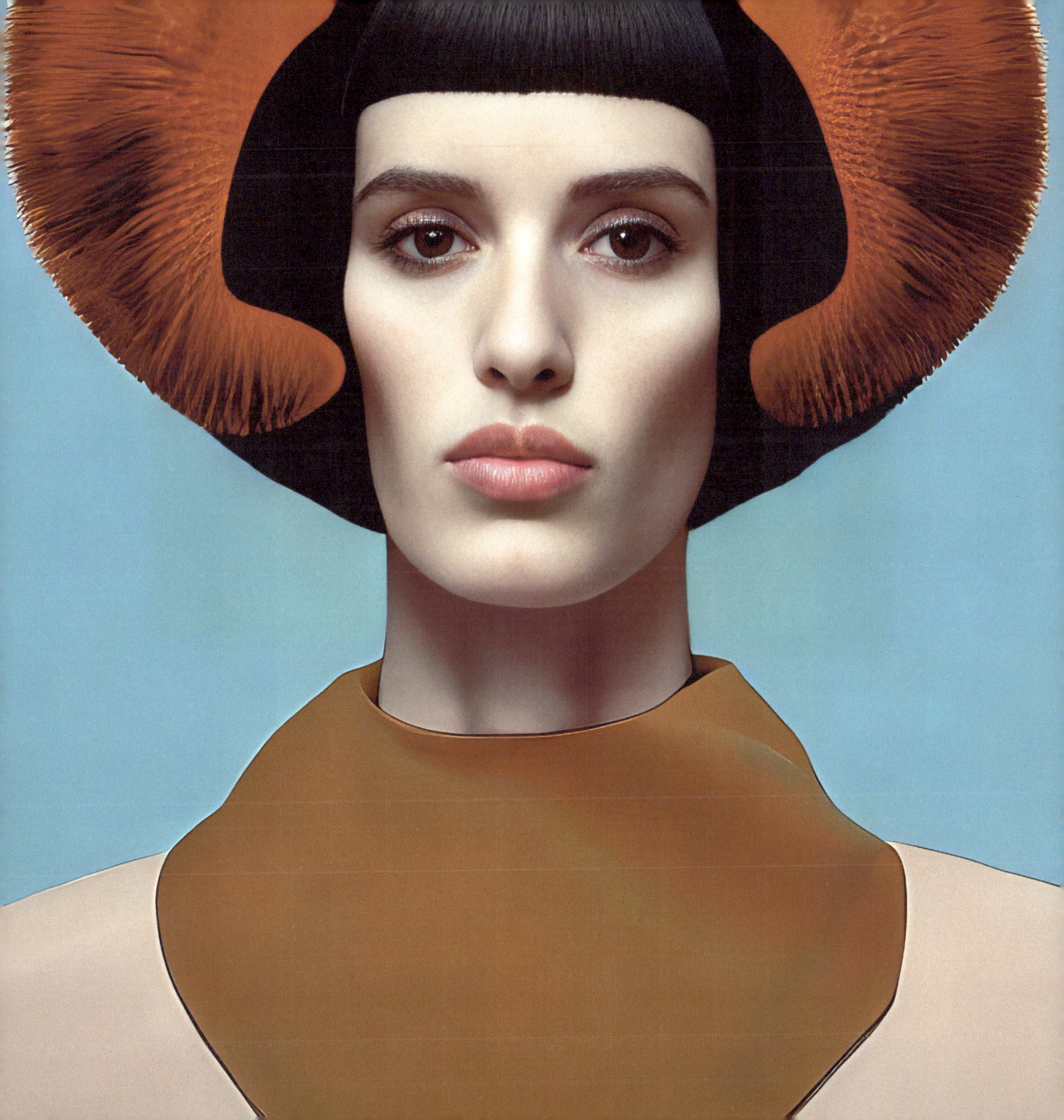

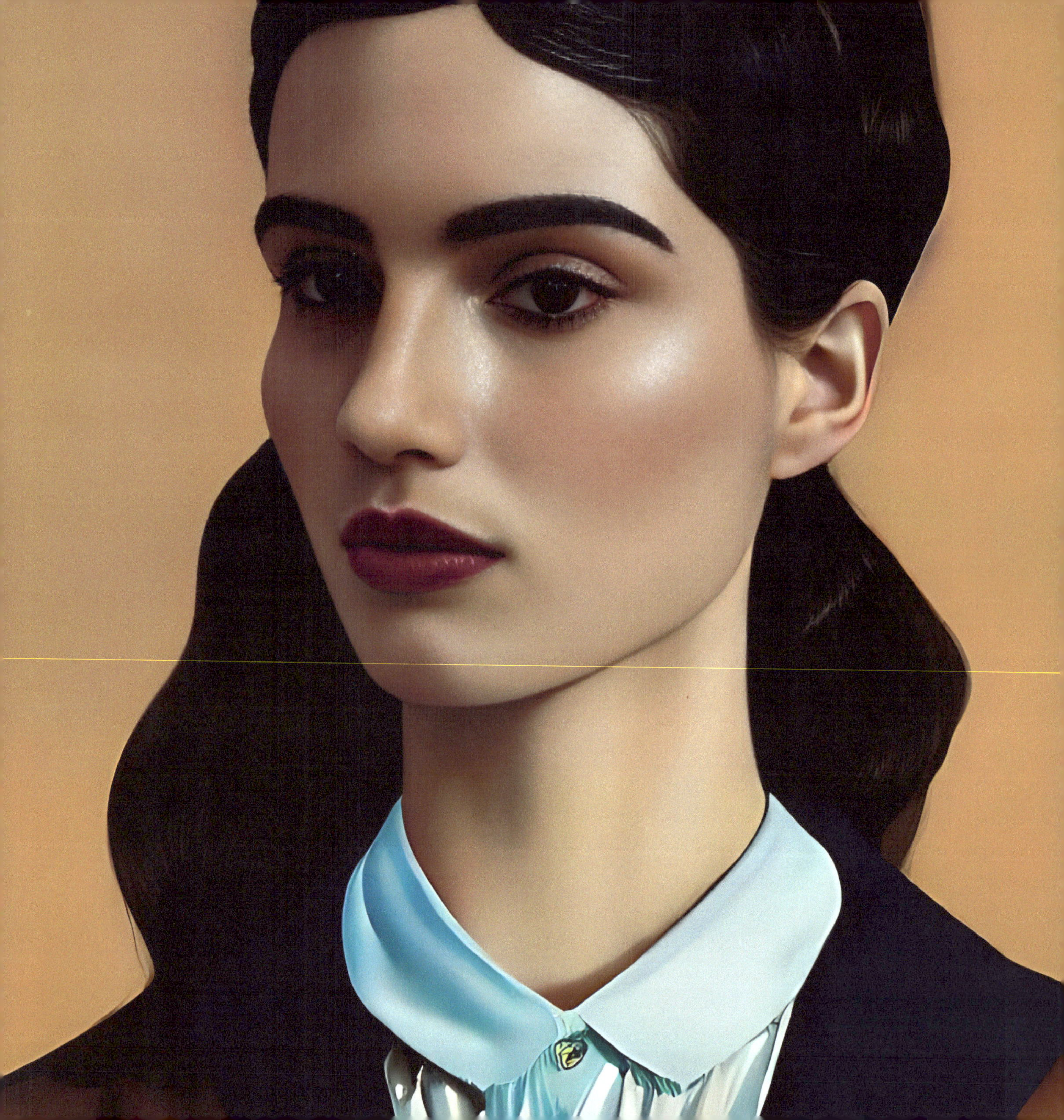

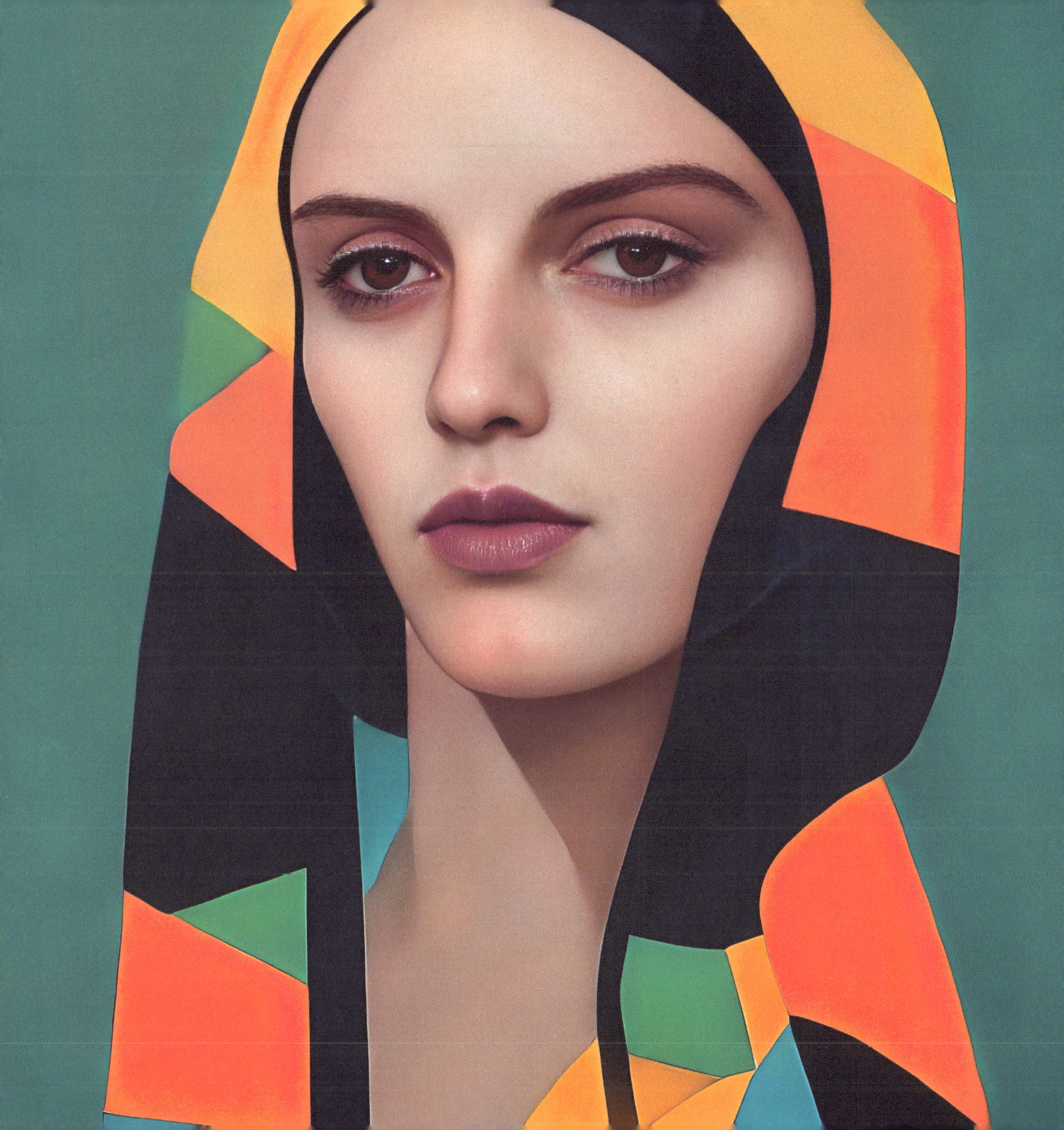

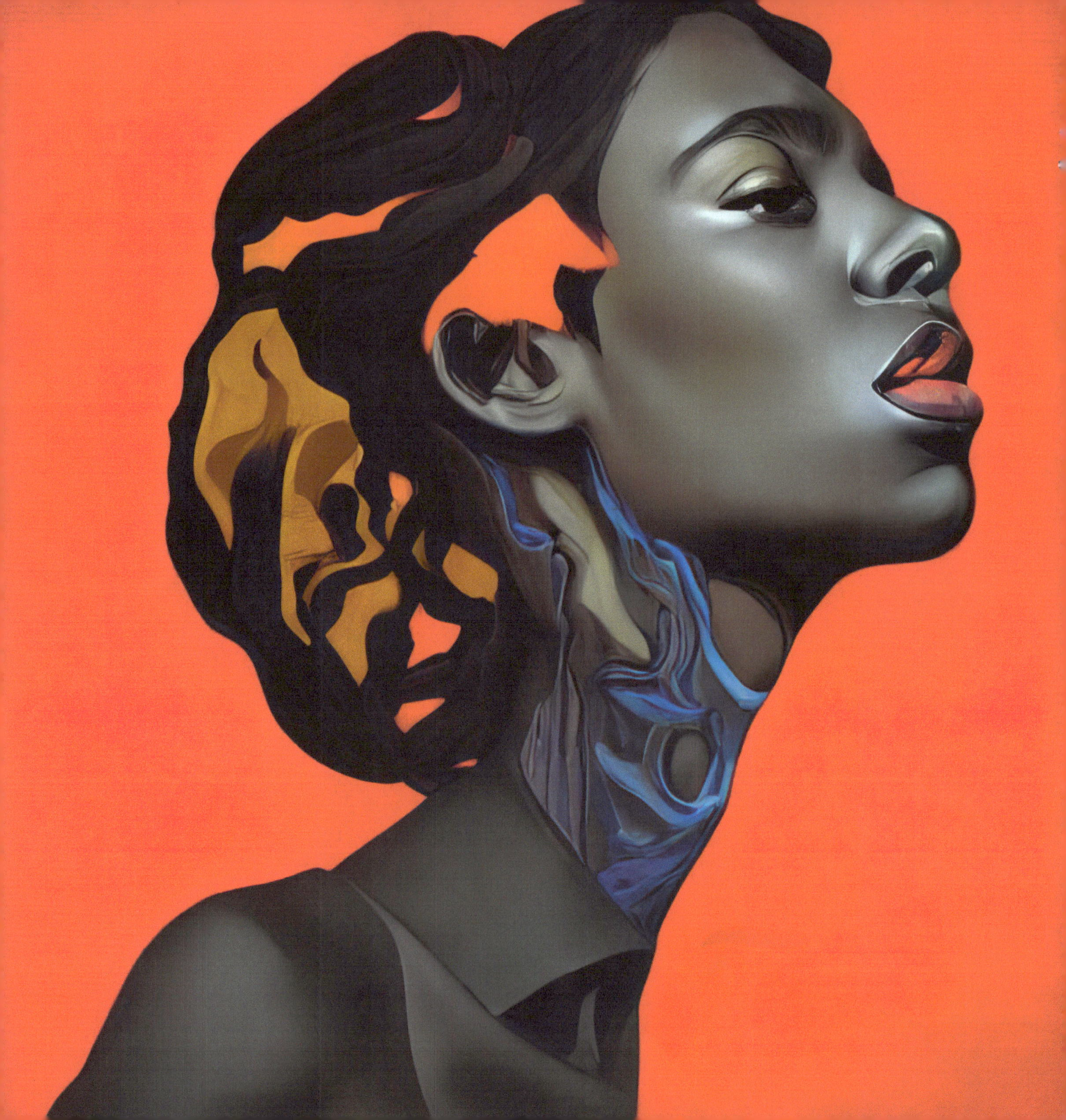

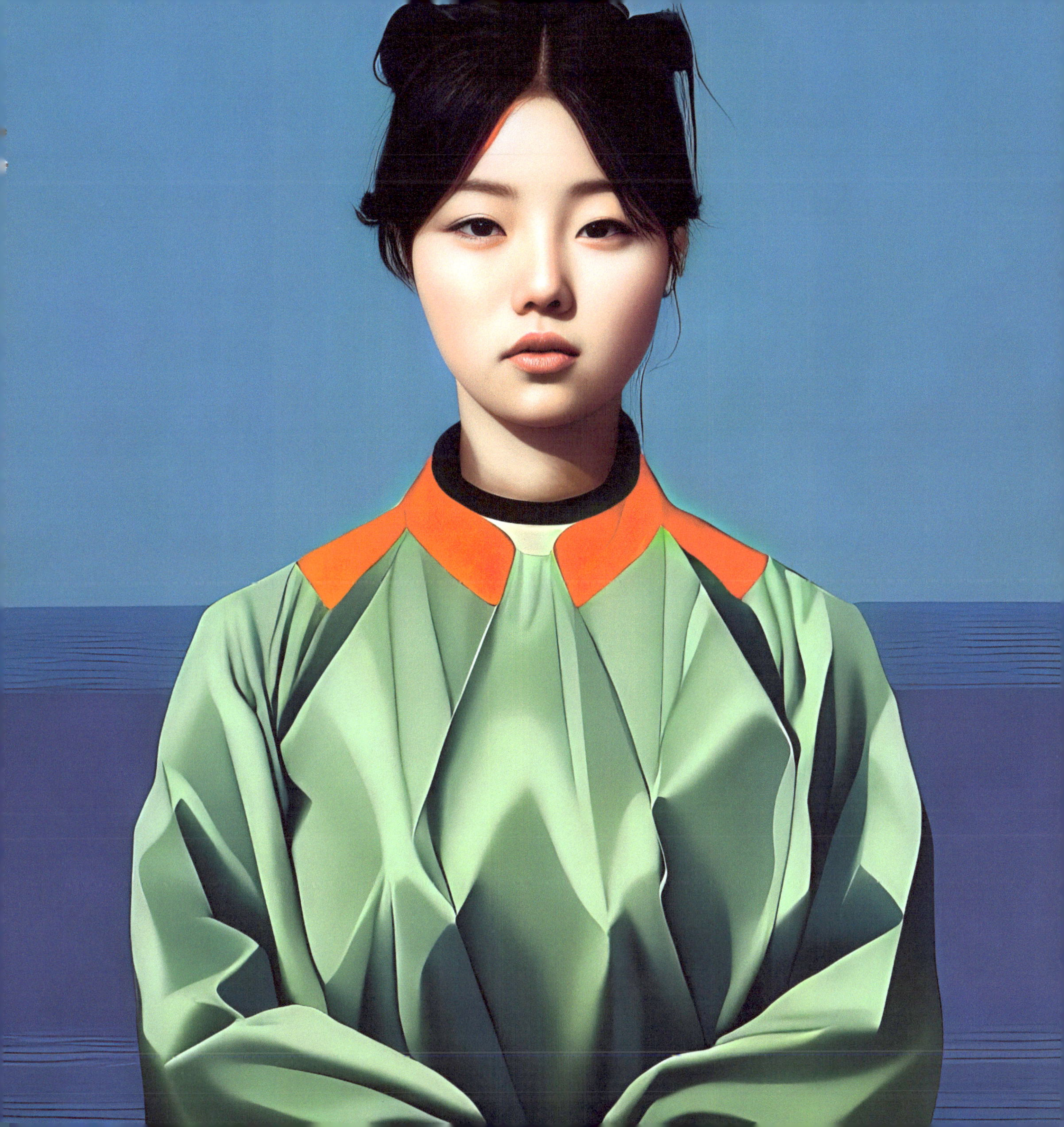

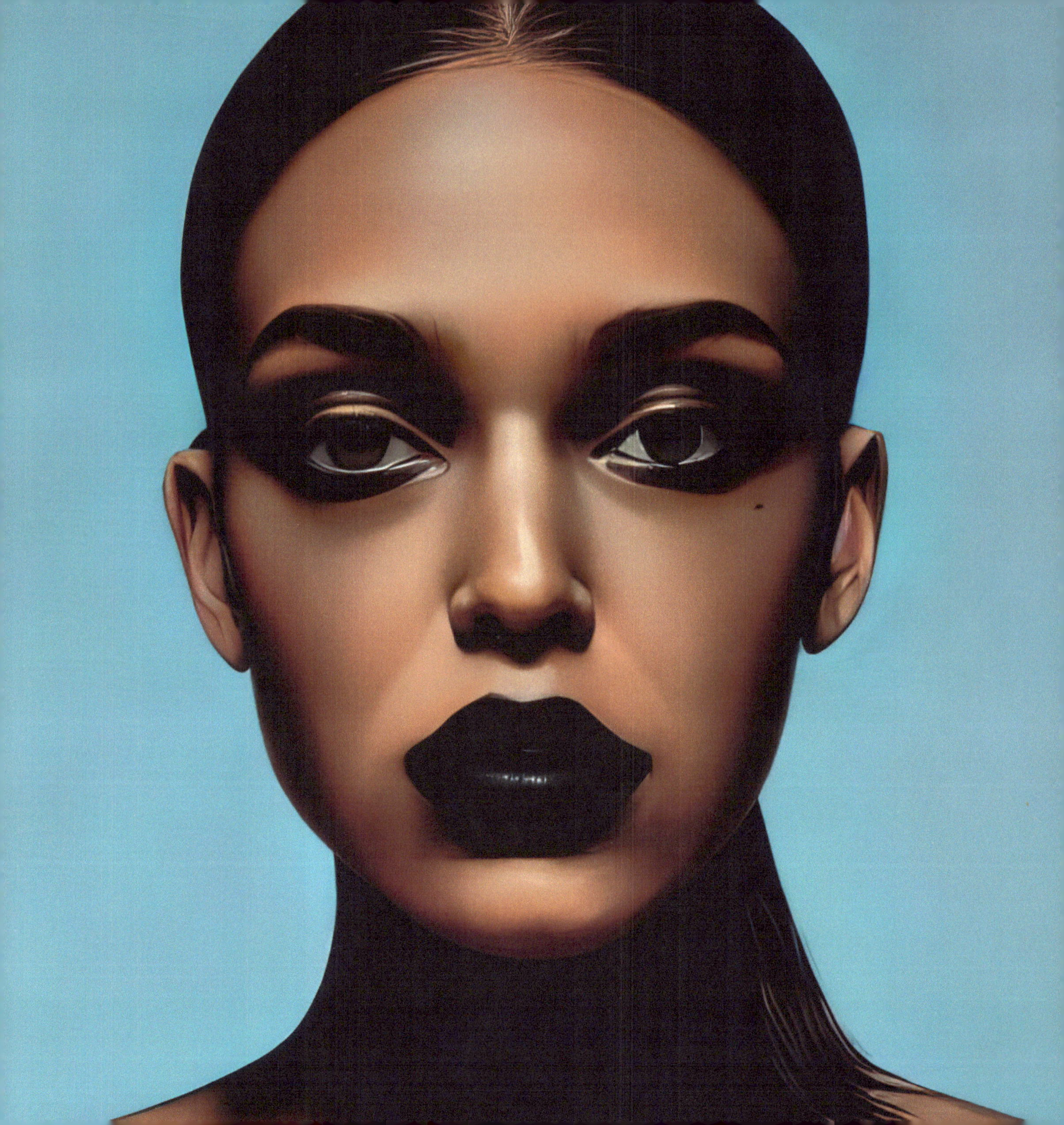

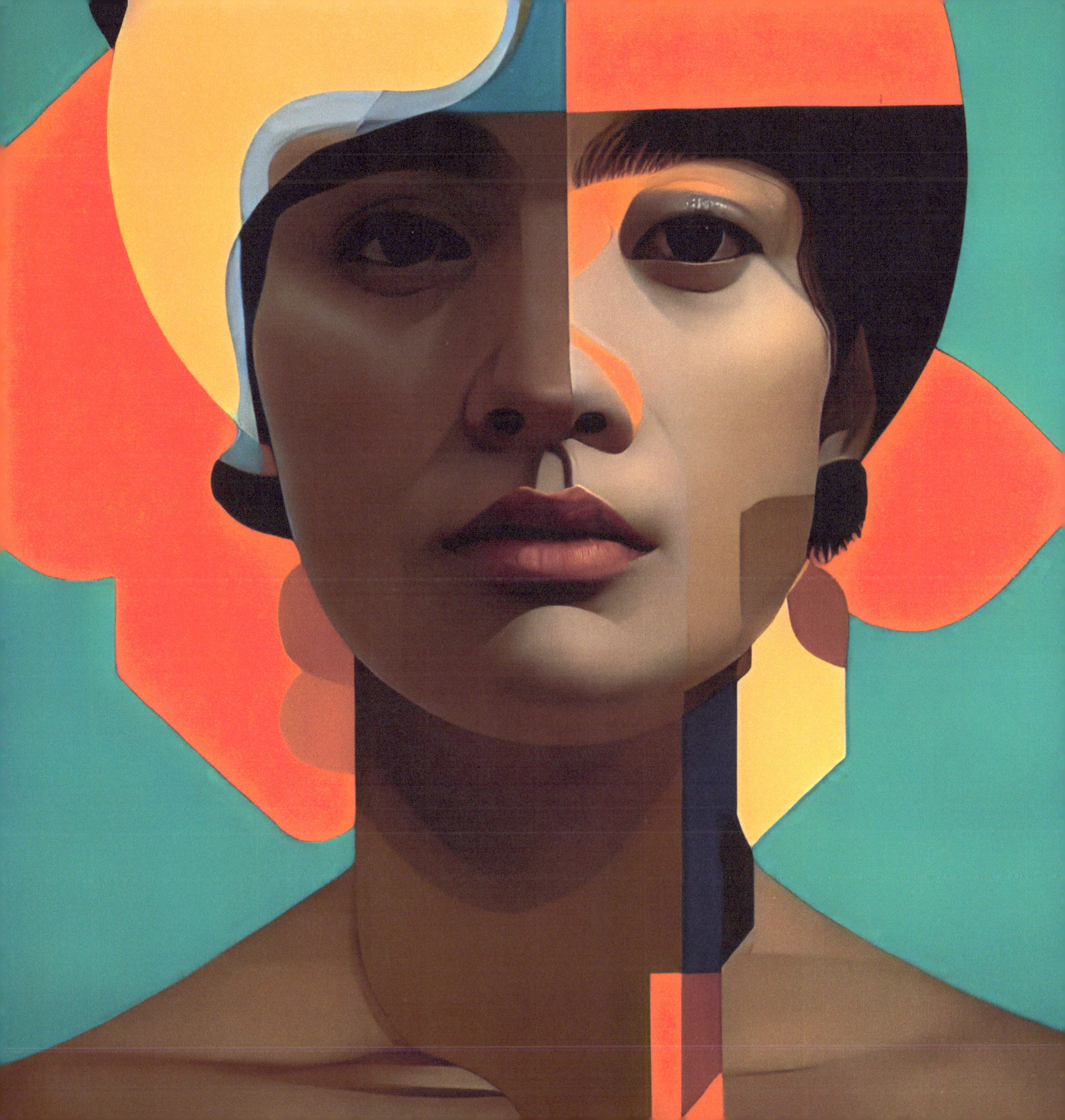

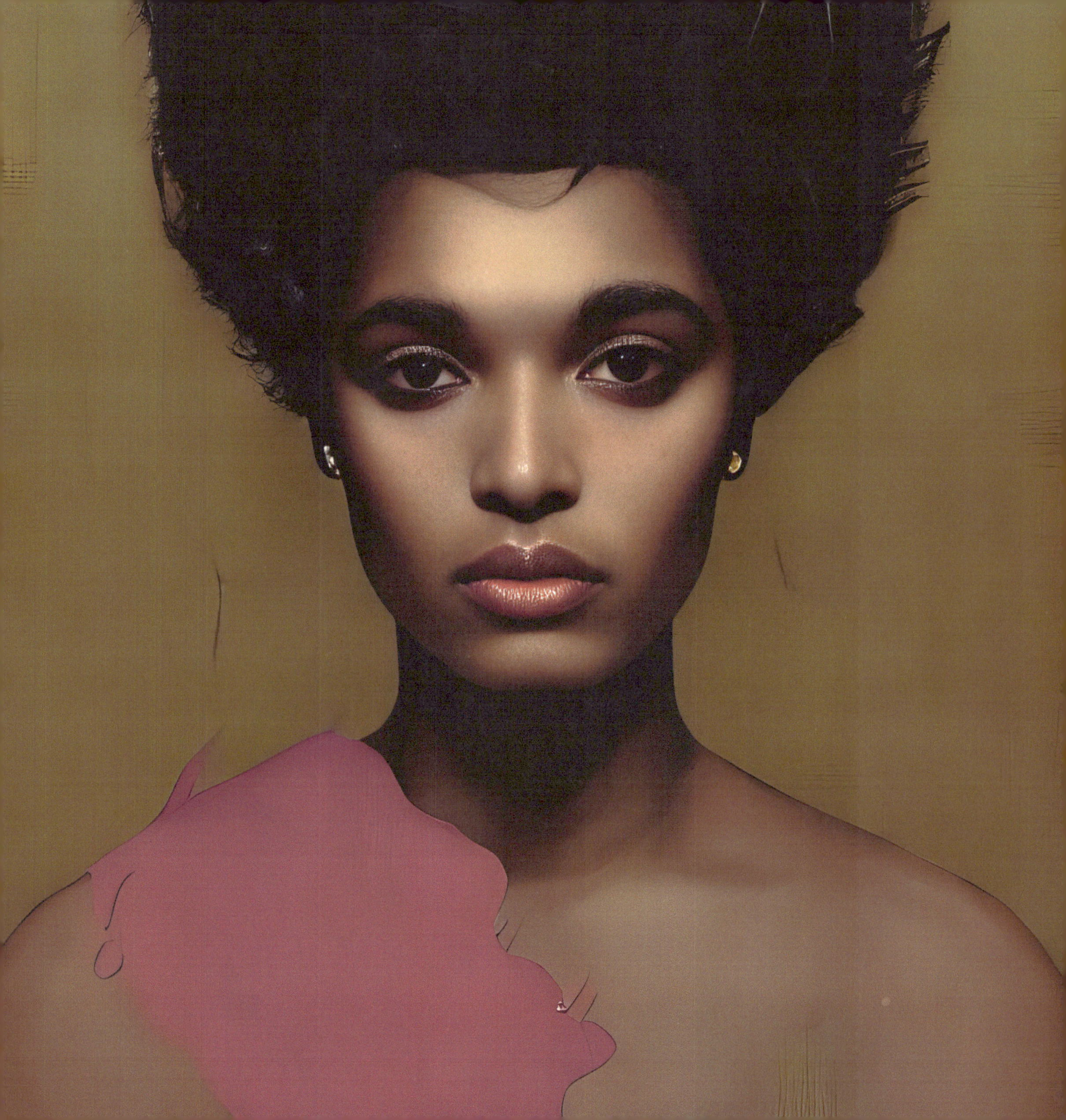

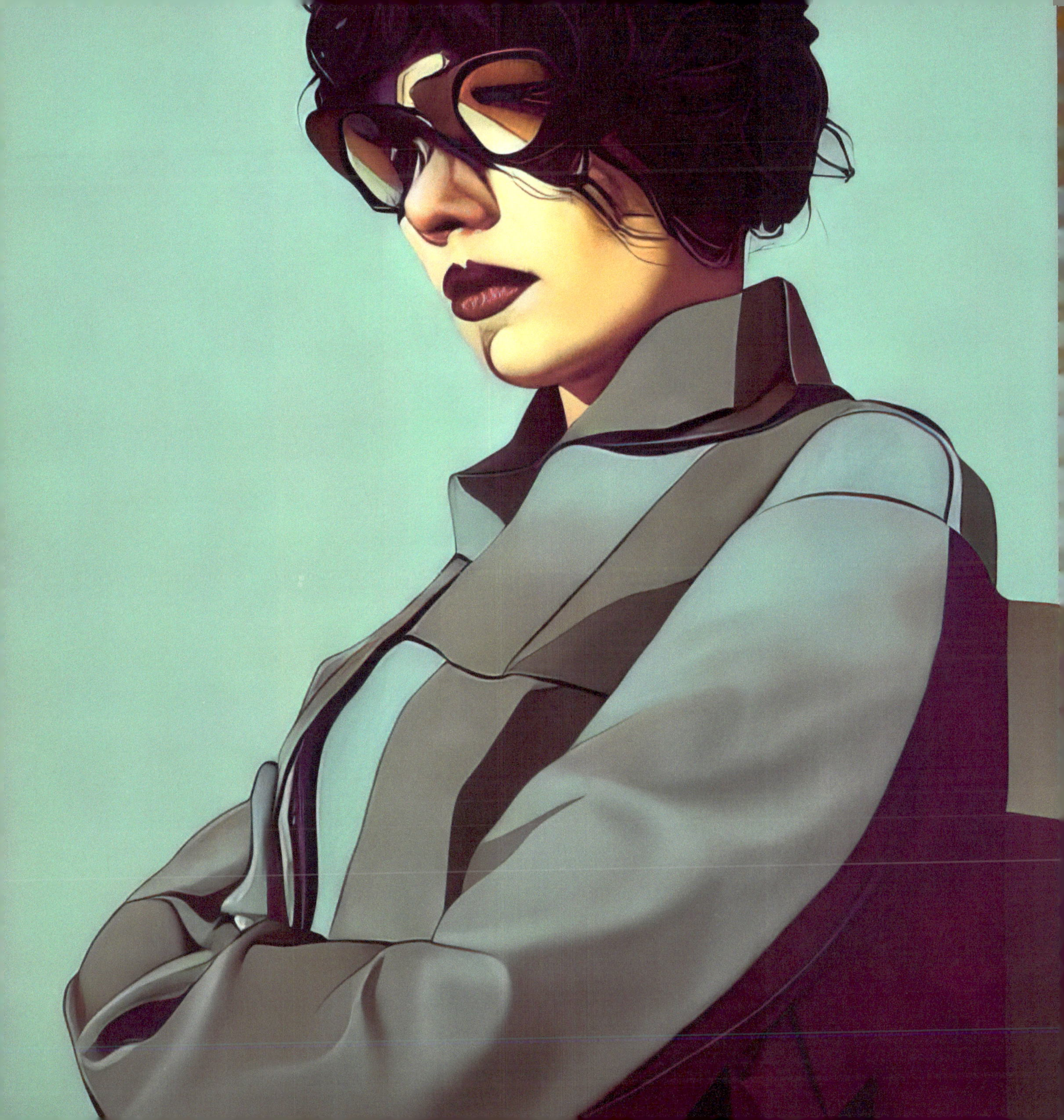

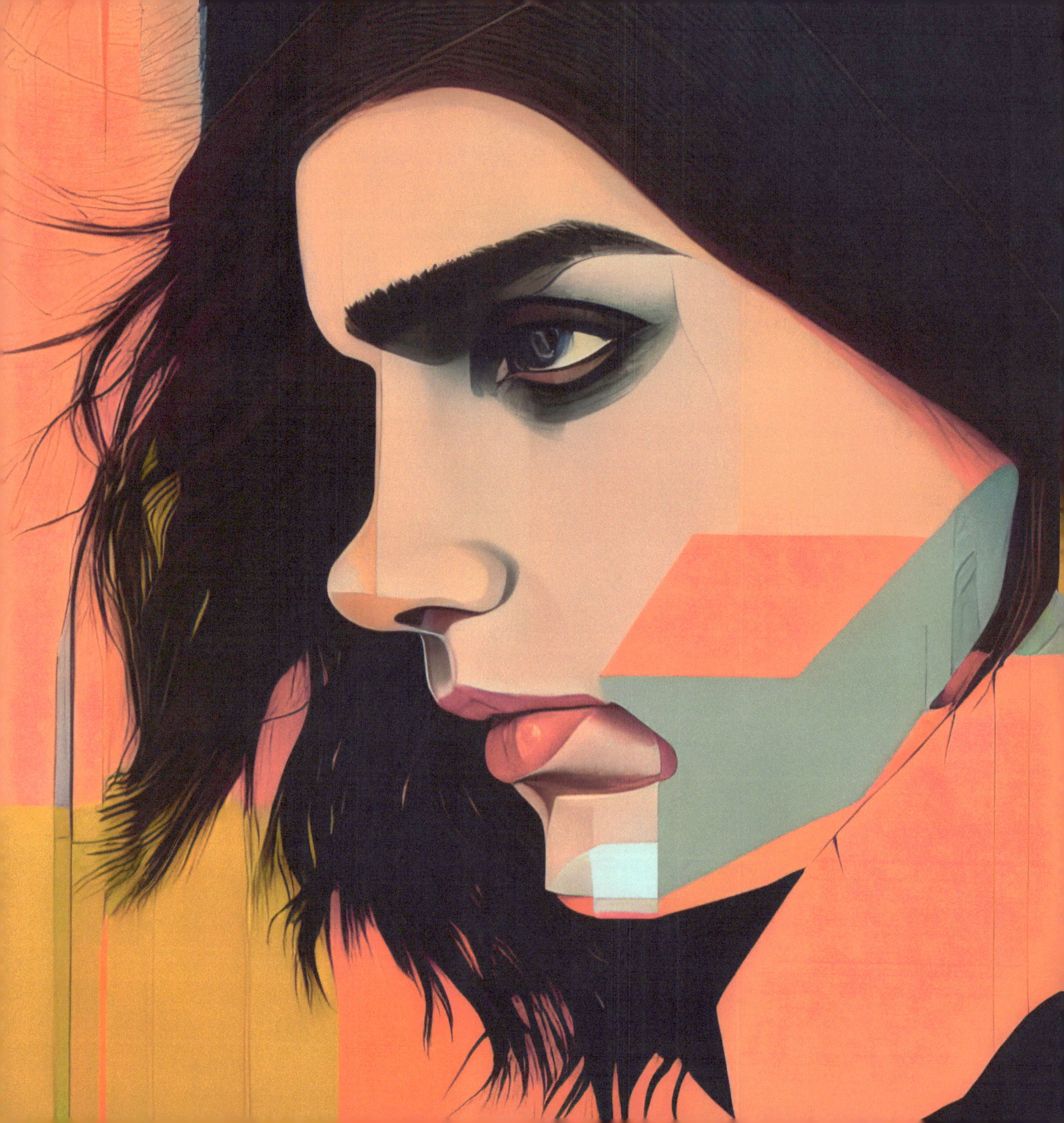

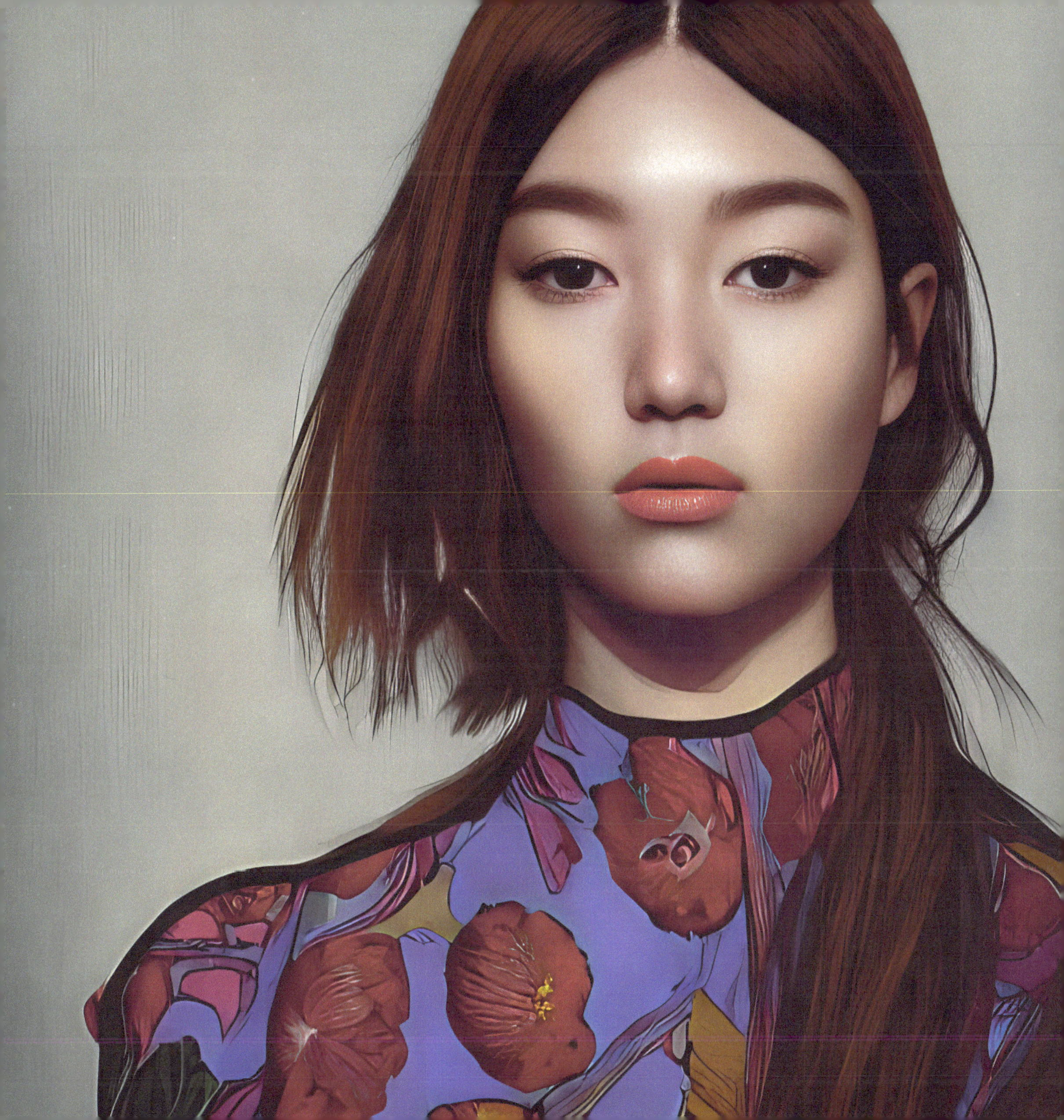

Conclusion

For centuries, artists have been at the forefront of pushing boundaries and expanding the way we see the world. Now, they find themselves on the cutting edge of another revolution: the emergence of Artificial Intelligence. Technology is becoming a significant source of inspiration for artists, and as A.I. continues to evolve, it is opening up new possibilities for creativity. As A.I. becomes more ubiquitous in our lives, these collaborations will become progressively influential in shaping our future.

In our daily lives, we increasingly intersect with Artificial Intelligence. From the automated voice that instructs us to leave a message at the beep to the predictive text that helps us compose emails and texts, A.I. is slowly but surely becoming a part of who we are. But what happens when humans and A.I. come face-to-face?

By tapping the power of generative A.I., artists can create works that would be impossible to produce without traditional methods. At the same time, generative A.I. algorithms are constantly learning and evolving, becoming better at making art that captures the unique perspective of their human creators. So far, generative A.I. has only scratched the surface of its potential. However, as this technology continues to develop, humans and A.I. will become increasingly intertwined, working together to create something greater than either could produce alone.

When it comes to generative A.I. art, it is one of the most fascinating and controversial applications. On the one hand, generative art can be seen as a form of creativity and expression. However, on the other hand, some argue that generative art is inherently different from traditional art because algorithms create it. They say that generative art expresses the machine's uniqueness rather than the human artist's individuality. But in this respect, generative art can be seen as a new form of expression rather than a copy of existing forms.

So far, generative art has mainly been exhibited in digital form. But as A.I. technology continues to develop, we will see more and more physical manifestations of generative art. For example, using Artificial Intelligence to create large-scale sculptures or paintings that are impossible for humans to make by hand. As generative art becomes more widespread, it will be interesting to see how people react to this new form of creativity.